# Glory of Arunachala

Translated *by*
M.C. Subramanian

Sri Ramanasramam
Tiruvannamalai 606 603
INDIA

| | | | |
|---|---|---|---|
| *First Edition* | *1999* | — | *1000 copies* |
| *Second Edition* | *2004* | — | *2000 copies* |
| *Third Edition* | *2006* | — | *2000 copies* |
| *Fourth Edition* | *2010* | — | *2000 copies* |
| *Fifth Edition* | *2013* | — | *2000 copies* |
| *Sixth Edition* | *2016* | — | *2000 copies* |
| Seventh Edition | 2019 | | |

2000 copies

CC No: 1098

**ISBN: 978-81-88018-31-4**

Price: ₹ 90

*Published by:*
**V.S. Ramanan**
President
SRI RAMANASRAMAM
Tiruvannamalai 606 603
Tamil Nadu, INDIA
*Email : ashram@gururamana.org*
*Web : www.sriramanamaharshi.org*

*Typeset at:*
Sri Ramanasramam

*Printed by:*
Prism Art Press
Chennai 600 028
Tamil Nadu, INDIA

# Publisher's Note

The Tamil translation of *Arunachala Mahatmyam* (Sanskrit) done by Sri Munagala S. Venkataramiah (later Sri Ramanananda Saraswati, compiler of *Talks with Sri Ramana Maharshi*) is already published by Sri Ramanasramam. The English translation of this by Sri M. C. Subramanian was serialised in *The Mountain Path.* This has been reissued now and includes a few alterations and additions. A long-felt need of devotees has at last been realised with the publication of this in book form.

An unavoidable feature of the original is the repetition of stories as compiled from various Sanskrit sources. This has been retained in translation in order to emphasise the glory of Arunachala as the main theme.

Appended to the *Arunachala Mahatmyam* (English), which forms the main body of the text, is the *Arunachala Puranam* as vignettes, translated by Sri J. Jayaraman from the Tamil poetic work of Saiva Ellappa Navalar, often referred to by Sri Bhagavan. This too originally appeared as a serial in *The Mountain Path.*

TIRUVANNAMALAI
1st September 1999

V. S. RAMANAN
PRESIDENT
SRI RAMANASRAMAM

# Contents

# PART - I

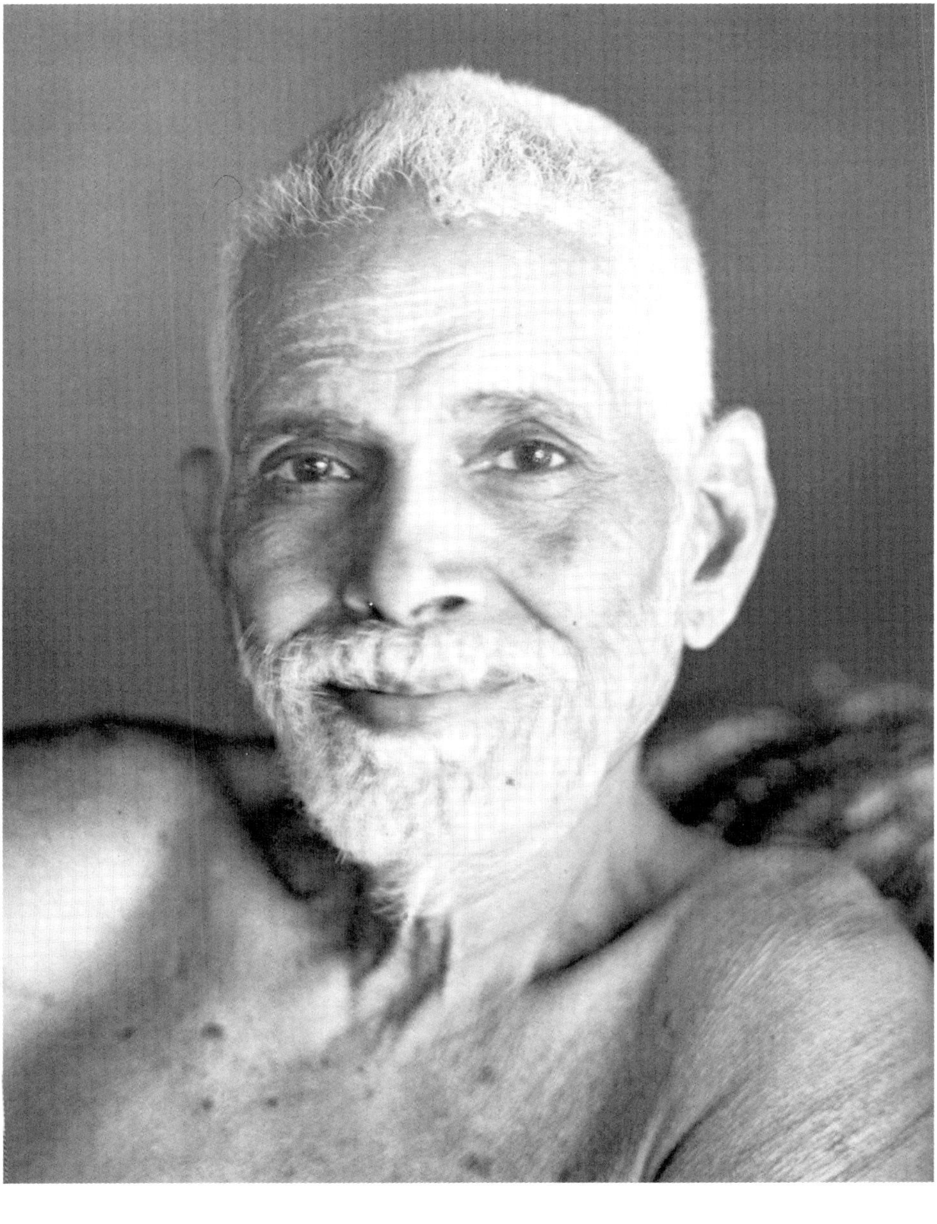

# INVOCATION

*Siva Mahimna Stotra*

O Hara! Even the words of Brahma and other Gods are inadequate to sing your Glory. It is therefore impossible for an ignorant man to speak of your greatness. Nevertheless, this, my deep desire to describe you as Indescribable, cannot be wrong.

Even the *Srutis* could only indirectly describe you as 'not this, not that', and your greatness as being beyond words and thought. How can one say what you are and who can visualise you? Yet, how can one remain without thinking or speaking of your revealed form? I am inclined to speak of your Glory so that I may become pure.

O Hill Supreme, when you stood as this Column of Effulgence, the utmost efforts of Brahma and Vishnu to realise your greatness were of no avail Later, full of devotion and faith, they praised you and you appeared before them! Can devotion fail to achieve anything?

# I. The Significance of Arunachala

IN the *Suta Samhita*, it is said: Siva's very form is *Linga*, hence the term, *Sivalinga*. Later it will be found that the Supreme Being revealed Himself as this *Linga* of Fire.

## Greatness of Sivalinga as told in the *Suta Samhita*

*Linga* is truly Siva. All is revealed by Siva who is the very essence of Consciousness and Knowledge. Nothing can reveal Him. Thus the *Linga* is the sole, Self-shining Reality. In brief, Siva is Consciousness Unmanifest, whereas *Sivalinga* is Consciousness Manifest.

Again it is said, that unto which all merge is the *Linga*. Everything is resolved into *Brahman*, but the Supreme *Brahman* being the sole Eternal Reality cannot merge into another. All but Siva merge into Siva. Therefore the *Linga* is Immortal Siva Himself. The whole universe is termed *Linga*, as the former is resolved and absorbed into and manifested from the latter. But the *Linga* is free from any emblem or characteristic mark.

This *Linga* is unqualified, beyond darkness. It is the source of the sacred syllable *Pranava* (OM). It is neither an entity nor a nonentity; neither the pervader nor the pervaded, neither the knowledge, nor the knower or the known; neither the manifest, the existing nor the unmanifest; neither real nor unreal, or a mixture of the two. It is only the Self-Realised. It illuminates all by its light; neither decaying nor undecaying; neither moving nor inert; neither the proof nor the proven; neither the vital air nor the mind; neither the seer nor the seen; neither the image nor its reflection; neither visible nor invisible; it is beyond speech and thought; it is not the eye, the ear, the nose, the earth, the ether, the vital airs or any object of the senses — to realise the Self, enquiring in this manner, is true worship.

This *Linga*, though not the ether nor different from it, yet reveals it; though not light, reveals it; though not air, yet makes it move; though not water, yet gives it its nature.

This *Linga* can be seen on a shining seat in the house of nine gates — never installed there by anyone but having faces, hands, feet, heads and seats in all directions. It lies beyond darkness; nothing can be seen there. It is revealed as the Unqualified Being by *Vedanta*. From it emerges the magnificent earth and is resolved into it. The three qualities namely, brightness, activity and darkness (*sattva*, *rajas* and *tamas*) of which the universe is made, manifests from it.

Its size cannot be estimated, for it has no magnitude. It remains unbroken and unitary. All the spheres of the vast universe are located in it. It has no temple but contains all in itself. It is the inmost core of all beings. It is neither *Isvara* nor the *jiva* but the Inmost Conscious Self, Bliss, Non-dual Reality unrelated to Brahma, Vishnu, Rudra, Indra etc. It can be realised only by the Self. It is the Self, known to oneself and abides within. This is the Supreme Bliss; there is nothing apart from it. It is always worshipped by all. It is free from the three states of waking, dream and deep sleep. It is *drik* — pure, beyond knowledge. Neither the ignorant nor the all-knowing individuals or gods in the power of the ego or *maya*, can see this *Linga*.

As this cannot be understood by all, out of His spontaneous infinite mercy, Siva is here manifest as Arunachala which all can see and worship.

# II. The Origin of the Hill

HERE at Arunachala, Siva shines forth as the *Yogi* Supreme, with his forehead smeared with three lines of sacred ashes and adorned by a patch of musk, clad in a loincloth, wearing a brilliant garland, the invincible serpent on his body and the crescent moon on his head.

Vyasa said: The holy men of Naimisaranya asked Suta: We desire to know from you about the greatness of Arunachala, please tell us. Suta thereupon described it as follows:

In former times Sanaka asked Brahma the same question. I shall repeat what Brahma narrated to Sanaka. Listen attentively. The sins of those who listen with faith to this narrative will be destroyed. Once upon a time Sanaka, with hands folded in salutation asked Brahma: O Creator of the Universe! Lord of the *devas*! Thou art known through the study of the Vedas! Four-faced One! I have by Thy grace acquired the ability to know everything. Thou art the Universal *Guru*. By Thy grace the knowledge of Siva (*Sivajnana*), the essence of the Vedas, has become clear. Ocean of Mercy! The divine *lingas* of Siva on earth, installed by human beings or *siddhas* are all of a concrete form. Kindly tell me which of these *lingas* found in the Island of Jambu (one of the nine islands or land masses into which the earth is divided according to Hindu mythology. India, situated in this island, is the purest, the best, Self-created, full of Effulgence and has the virtue of destroying desire, anger, greed, delusion, pride and jealousy). Ocean of Compassion! Kindly tell me as to which of these can, by merely thinking of it, destroy all sins and grant the eternal state of Siva. Please enlighten me about that *linga* which is the primal cause of the world and which truly represents the imperishable splendour of Siva and the sight of which makes one feel that the supreme aim of life has been fulfilled.

On hearing these eager words of Sanaka, Brahma was pleased. Sitting on the lotus he meditated on Sambhu (another name for Siva) for a long time and was immersed in bliss. In this state he had a vision of Siva as He had formerly revealed Himself as a Column of Light. The four-faced Brahma lost awareness of the surroundings. By Siva's Grace and on His instructions, Brahma emerged from his trance and noticed Kumara (literally the son, Sanaka) standing in a worshipful attitude. With hair standing on end and with tears of joy brought forth by the vision of Siva, he spoke in a faltering voice: O Son! You have made me remember the ancient *yoga* of Siva. You have developed supreme devotion to Siva as a result of great austerities. Those pure souls who possess unceasing devotion to the Eternal Siva purify the entire world by their lives. To talk, associate or sport with devotees of Siva removes all sins; even mere remembrance or sight of them removes all sins.

Now I shall describe how Siva, the Ocean of Grace, manifested as Arunachala, the Light of Consciousness. From the Supreme Effulgence which is the Eternal Siva, Narayana (Vishnu) and I were born in accordance with His desire. Both of us manifested spontaneously. Once, out of egoism, we engaged in an argument and started a fight. Seeing the terrible rage into which we had fallen while quarrelling, the Lord reflected: Why should there be a destructive fight between these two, as to who is greater? If I do not reveal myself immediately to both and stop their fight, the world will cease to exist. These two who have in their anger lost their senses, do not know the *Vedic* truth that my glory transcends everything. Each creature considers itself superior to every other creature. The ignorant who cannot realize and concede equality or superiority of another must necessarily suffer defeat and fall. I shall reveal myself in a definite form somewhere in the world, so that even a mean human being can attain me the moment he thinks of me.

Having so decided, the Eternal Siva manifested Himself as a Column of fire before us. The Column transcended all the worlds and its limits could not be perceived. Blinded by the sight, both of us stood still. We became confused and unnerved on seeing that blazing Column of Effulgence. Then there arose a voice in the air: Children, why do you fight? Siva alone knows your strength and weakness. The form of Sambhu has now appeared before you as a Column of Effulgence. He who finds out the beginning or the end of it is the greater of the two.

Upon hearing these words we stopped fighting. To discover the limits of Sambhu in the shape of a beginningless and endless Column of fire, one of us decided to trace the beginning and the other the end. Like a child who tries to seize the moon reflected in water, each of us began to measure the Supreme Effulgence in order to understand it. For this purpose, Vishnu in the form of a huge boar began to dig the earth vigorously to find the lower end. I took the shape of a swan and soared swiftly to find its summit. Madhava (Vishnu) bored into the earth and went beyond, but found that the Column of fire went still lower. Even after seeking for millions of years it was not possible to find out the source of that beginningless Column of fire. Therefore Vishnu became dispirited and discouraged. He was weary and tired and he was forced to return.

Then Vishnu, whose intelligence is immeasurable, sought refuge in Siva, the Universal Refuge and began to think thus: Ah! On account of my immense stupidity caused by my ego I forgot the Supreme Self, my Lord. He is truly the Supreme Siva, the source of all the *devas*, the

Vedas and the worlds. I was born out of Him who is beginningless and endless. Assuming the form of a brute I tried to gauge Siva who is of such greatness. By the Grace of Sambhu, Self-knowledge has dawned on me. When Lord Sambhu chooses to protect someone, the person will immediately and spontaneously lose his ego and gain wisdom. I am no longer strong enough to worship the Universal *Guru.* Therefore I shall surrender unto Him. Vishnu praised Siva in this manner, meditated upon Him, and by the Grace of the Lord, he regained the surface of the earth.

As for me, I was flying for many years until my eyes became dim and my wings tired. The splendid Effulgence of Siva in the form of a *linga* of Light rose higher and higher. *Siddhas* who found me trying to reach the immeasurable top of the Supreme Effulgence exclaimed: Ah! this is nothing but ignorance. He is still putting forth his efforts. Even when the body is about to fall the ego does not fade away. Even though his wings are broken and weary and his eyes dim, he is bound by the vain delusion that he can discover the limits of the limitless Effulgence. Vishnu who became similarly despondent, regained good sense by Siva's spontaneous grace and retraced his steps. If a finite being desires to realize the Effulgence which is the origin of Brahma and the *devas,* he should dive within himself and meditate on Siva, the Supreme Self, who will give him knowledge so that his ego will vanish. On hearing these kind words I became humble and began to reflect thus:

Knowledge of Siva can be attained only through Siva's Grace, not through the Vedas, nor austerities, nor dips in holy waters. Even though my wings are tired and my limbs too weak to move, my mind desires to nourish the ego. Alas! Always active and dependant upon the strength of the non-self, I have become despicable. My salutations to the *siddhas* who have fixed their minds upon Siva. I shall associate with them and perform austerities. I shall turn my mind inwards and realize this Effulgence of Siva which appears in front of me. The *devas* have conquered their enemies by worshipping Siva and have crowned themselves with glory. Even the great *Vedic mantras* do not throw light on His Reality. Therefore I shall seek refuge with Siva. I came into being through devotion to Siva who wears the crescent moon. Ah! How strange that with the egos born of Siva, both Vishnu and I fought each other, and that Sankara Himself revealed His greatness and humbled our pride! He who worships the Eternal Siva, who is the Lord worshipped by the *devas* as this column of Light of Consciousness, realizes Siva, and serves as a boat to cross the ocean of *samsara*.

# III

# Parvathi's Penance at Kanchi

SANAKA addressed Brahma thus: O Bhagavan! Having obtained the grace of Siva through you, it has been possible for me to hear with joy the glory of Arunachala. I now understand that the beginningless and endless Siva himself stands as the Aruna Hill in order to grant the devotee the fruits of his penance, that the Hill destroys all sins and that one obtains Liberation by merely uttering 'Arunachala' once. All desires are fulfilled when one stands before it. All tendencies (*vasanas*) are destroyed. The very name 'Siva' is nectar. Repeating the name is itself worship of Siva. Pray, tell me, who else worshipped Arunachala, the bestower of boons?

On hearing this, Brahma, the Lord of the celestial beings, mentally prayed to the Lord of Arunachala, the embodiment of compassion, and resumed his narrative:

# 15

Child! I shall now narrate how in days of yore, the Universal Mother, Goddess Parvati sought and won the left-half of Her Lord, Arunachala. Once on Mount Kailas, it was spring time and the place was filled with the balm, incense and scent of beautiful flowers. Bees swarmed and hummed among the hanging clusters of flowers. Peacocks spread out their colourful feathers dancing to the tune of humming bees. Elephants and lions, natural enemies, strolled about in harmony and contentment. Sages chanted hymns from the Rig, the Yajus and the Sama Vedas, the last mentioned being most dear to Siva. *Brahmarishis* and *Rajarishis* were deeply absorbed in the Self, while *devas*, *siddhas*, *ganas*, the protectors of the quarters and holy devotees of Siva wearing sacred ash and *rudraksha* beads stood in prayerful attitude. Hosts of *Apsaras* (celestial damsels) sang and danced to the accompaniment of the sweet-sounding *veena* (a stringed musical instrument), the *venu* (the flute), the *mridangam* (a small drum) and other musical instruments. Lord Siva and Parvati, the Universal Parents, sat on their throne in all their glory, pouring their Grace on their children who were worshipping them.

*Devas*, *rishis* and other hosts of devotees, after being granted the boons they desired, prayerfully took leave of their Lord. Now Lord Siva rejoiced in the company of Goddess Uma (Parvati) on the snow-clad peaks of the Himalayan mountains. A cool and refreshing breeze from the rivers below wafted gently, carrying with it the sweet scent of flowers from the plains. In a joyous mood the

Goddess, who thought that Her Lord's attention was entirely centred on Her, slipped behind Him and playfully covered the three eyes of Sambhu with Her lotus-like hands, and asked, 'Tell me, who is it?'

As soon as the three eyes representing the Moon, the Sun and the Fire of Knowledge were covered, a dismal darkness spread over the universe. It lasted for millions of years because half a moment for Siva is aeons for us. The darkness produced by the playfulness of the Goddess proved to be the cause of the untimely dissolution of the worlds, for in the dense darkness no activities were possible and consequently, living beings perished without giving birth to new generations. The *devas* became inert and the Vedas could not be chanted. By this unforeseen darkness cause and effects were nullified. Seeing this state of affairs, the ever glorious *siddhas* by their *yogic* powers discovered the cause, but could not comprehend the divine play of the Lord.

The *siddhas* prayed to Sambhu with devotion and addressed Him thus: "Glory to Sambhu, the origin of the universe and the Supreme Immanent Being. The power (*sakti*) which is not apart from you sportfully creates, sustains and dissolves the universe. She (Sakti) is half of you. Siva and Sakti together constitute a single form. The great Lord is One. There is nothing different from you. An untimely deluge has now overtaken the worlds on account of the Goddess' sport. But your compassion is infinite. May it reveal itself now for the well-being of the universe. Therefore, O Sadasiva! (Eternal Siva), Kala!

(Embodiment of time), Embodiment of Compassion! Be merciful. Pray, stop this sport!

In response to this prayer of devotees and *siddhas*, Siva commanded: 'Gowri! Leave my eyes alone'. Immediately the Goddess removed Her hands from Siva's eyes. Light pervaded the worlds. On asking the *siddhas* who stood in an attitude of worship, as to how much time had elapsed, they replied, 'Half a second for Thee, but millions of years for us.' On hearing this the Lord turned with a smile to his beloved and graciously spoke some words on *dharma* and *artha*: 'Gowri, how can you be so thoughtless! You who are the Mother of the world have been the cause for its dissolution. O, how can you, the very embodiment of love and compassion, cause pain to your children?'

On hearing Sambhu's words of reproach, Uma, stricken with remorse, pleaded with Him to advise Her as to the course to be adopted for expiation of this fault of hers. At this Lord Siva was pleased with the repentance and devotion of the Goddess and said: 'What penance can you perform without me? All *dharma, Srutis* (Vedas), *Smritis* (scriptures based on the Vedas), *karmas* (rituals), *kalpas* (code of virtues), various branches of learning, the *devas*, etc., are all your forms only. You who symbolise my power and who desire to recreate the world are not different from myself. Goddess! The timeless Vedas declare you to be the All. Therefore I shall prescribe a penance for you in accordance with prevailing practice. I cannot remain without you even for a moment. Being the universal Self, I shall myself go through the austerities. Let the entire world become sacred by the glory of your penance. People will be relieved of all troubles by surrendering at your lotus feet. By having your *darshan* when you perform austerities and by association with you they (the devotees) will get sanctified. May you perform meritorious acts for the welfare of all creation. People will acquire firm faith in *dharma* by seeing you performing penance. There is no doubt about it. Your grace shall sustain the earth and its *dharma*.

'The city known as Kanchipuri is heaven on earth. A little penance done there yields boundless results. Even *devas*, saints and others desire to live there. There flows the holy river, the Kampa which washes away the sins of all the people living in its vicinity. At that place there is a divine mango tree which is always shady, full of leaves and fruit. *Homas* (fire offerings), *japas* (repetition of sacred names), and the least good action performed under its shade yield boundless merit. May the many groups of celestial beings headed by Vishnu surround and worship you. I shall also remain there in the lotus of your heart in my formless state as the Absolute Pure Being. Therefore you need not suffer the pangs of separation from me.'

On hearing this the Goddess with Her companions proceeded at once to the holy city of Kanchipuram situated on the banks of the Kampa to do penance. There She saw the pure and holy waters of the Kampa worshipped by hosts of sages and a magnificent mango tree full of fruits and flowers among which koels sang and sported. Amidst such a beautiful setting the Goddess meditated on Her

Lord. Her body tortured by the pang of separation from Her Lord, immediately became emaciated as if She had been performing penance for a long time. Turning to Vijaya, one of the maids who stood near Her, Goddess Gowri, in uncontrollable sorrow spoke thus: 'Those who perform austerities with the object of worshipping Siva directly seek this sin-destroying mango tree and always live here. This well-known *Ekamra* (*lit.*, a mango tree which bears just a single fruit) increases my pain of separation. How am I to bear this? The sure remedy for this must be to remember and concentrate in the heart on Chandramouleeswara (the wearer of the crescent moon).'

At this Vijaya bowed devotedly to Ambika and praised Siva fervently in order that the Goddess regain Her composure.

She said: 'Oh Devi! You will not be abandoned by Siva at any time. For, you are His very life and the Supreme Sakti. It is only when you desire to spread out your *maya* (power of illusion), that the Lord, though always one with you, appears to be separate. You have come here at the command of Sambhu to worship Him and you cannot transgress it. You may perform *tapas* in this temple erected by Siva without any rituals (*karmas*). Moreover, as you are yourself the world, the protection of the world is in your power. You will again join Siva and uphold *dharma*. That being so, Parvati, how can you feel the pain of separation? Devotee of *dharma*, may your religious observances become known to the world and set an example to your devotees.'

On hearing her maid speak thus, Gowri continued to practise austerities on the banks of the Kampa. She discarded Her fine clothes and ornaments and wore the bark of a tree as garment and beads of *rudraksha*. Her entire body was smeared with sacred ash. She subsisted on corn picked by herself. The name of Siva was always on Her lips. Thrice a day She bathed in the Kampa, lovingly shaped its sand into a *linga* and devoutly worshipped it with leaves as traditionally prescribed. The Goddess observed the *dharma* of alleviating the misery of all creatures thus showering Her compassion on Her children. In summer She surrounded herself with fire, lay on the bare ground in the rainy season and stood in ice-cold water in winter. She respectfully welcomed the holy sages (*Maharshis*) who came to pay homage to Her. The sages were struck with wonder at Her austerities.

One day, Parvati collected flowers from the forest and began to worship a *linga* made of sand on the bank of the Kampa. Siva, to reveal to the world Her devotion to Him, made the waters of the river Kampa suddenly rise and overflow its banks. Seeing the spate of the river, Her companions raised an alarm, whereupon the Devi opened Her eyes and saw the approaching flood. Distressed at the danger to Her worship, She at once embraced the *linga* lest it dissolve. She then addressed Her maids, 'What is to be done? Worship ought not be discontinued, come what may. In this world, only those blessed ones who have acquired merit can reap the benefits of their good deeds and establish *dharma* which is capable of fulfilling one's desires. This

*Sivalinga* is made of sand. It will dissolve in this flood. Should this happen, a true devotee of the Lord cannot bear it. This flood has risen through the *maya* of Siva to test the sincerity of my devotion. I shall continue without the least fear. Friends! Go away quickly!' Saying this, Parvati though surrounded by the fast rising waters, devoutly adored the *linga* clasped to Her breast and with open eyes meditated on Sadasiva with one-pointed devotion.

Then a divine voice was heard: O child, noblest of beings! This great flood has subsided. You can now let go of the *linga*. This *linga* worshipped by you will achieve everlasting fame as the one worshipped by the gods and will be capable of granting boons. May your penance be successful! May the human beings who have *darshan* and worship this *linga* installed for the upkeep of *dharma* attain their lives' goal! I myself shine on this earth in the form of the Effulgent Arunachala for the liberation of mortals. The name signifies that the accumulated sins of the worlds will completely vanish at the sight of it. *Rishis, siddhas, gandharvas, yogis,* etc., come to Arunachala and fervently worship it, forsaking even the peaks of Kailash and Mount Meru. You may go there and learn from the Sage Gautama about devotion to me and the glory of Arunachala and perform further penance. I shall reveal to you my Effulgent form there in order that all sins of the world may be destroyed and may prosper.

On hearing these words of Siva, the Devi said, "So be it", and got ready to leave at once for Arunachala. Turning to the *rishis* who desired to follow Her, She said,

"*Devas! Rishis* resolute in religious observances! Remain where you are. Perform your austerities on the bank of the sacred Kampa. This *linga* of sand which removes all sins and brings all kinds of prosperity bears the marks of my embrace. Worship it. Let my devotees know that I shall be known as Kamakshi as I fulfil all their desires and bless them. Let them also worship me and obtain the boons they desire. I am entirely under the control of Sambhu, the Lord of the *devas*. I shall therefore go to Arunachala and carry out His command. After I have performed penance there and obtained the grace of Sambhu you may come and see me."

# IV. Gowri Arrives at Arunachala

AS narrated previously, Gowri at Her Lord's bidding came to Arunachala. There She worshipped with great fervour the Effulgent Lord along with with Her companions to the sound of divine *dundhubis* accompanied by the dancing of *apsaras*. As a result of worshipping the motionless *Linga* in such a rigorous manner She became emaciated.

On arrival, the Goddess saw *siddhas*, *yogis*, *rishis* and *devas* dwelling there. The *devas* said, "Atri, Bhrigu, Bharadwaja, Kasyapa, Angirasa, Kutsa, Gautama and *siddhas*, *vidhyadharas* and *devas* perform severe penances here for the fulfillment of their wishes. The Ganga and other sacred rivers worship this *Linga*-Hill. This is the noble and divine *Linga* known as Arunadri."

The *Maharshis* prayed to Her to be their guest, but She expressed Her desire to see Gautama first, as per Siva's command. So they directed Her to his *ashram*.

Gautama, foremost among sages, had gone out into the forest in the morning to procure flowers and other articles for worship. Devi went to his hermitage where She was received by his disciples with great respect and hospitality. With humility they entreated Her to wait a little for the sage and sat around Her.

Gautama returning from the forest with paraphernalia used for performing rituals, saw from a distance his *ashram* glow in resplendent beauty and wondered as to its cause. He then divined through his *yogic* powers that this was due to the arrival of Gowri. He hastened with great eagerness and joy to welcome the Mother of the Universe. His disciples came to meet him and informed him about Gowri's arrival. The elated Maharshi foresaw in the visit of the Goddess the fruition of his austerities.

Goddess Gowri came forward to welcome Gautama. Years of rigorous *tapas* had endowed him with a radiant countenance. Sporting a flowing white beard and red-brown *rudraksha* beads, smeared with sacred ash and clad in bark, the sage reached the frontyard of the *ashram* chanting *Vedic mantras* dear to Rudra. His voice was deep and resonant, and his words brimmed with love and compassion like that of Siva himself. The Sage resembled the sun, such was his lustre and benevolence. On seeing this great sage coming with his band of disciples, Uma, full of divine grace, Her slim body resembling a creeper folded Her hands respectfully and made obeisance to the Sage. When Gautama saw the Mother of the worlds bowing to him, he restrained Her from doing so and himself bowed to Her. He said: 'Gowri! Welcome! Auspicious Mother of the Universe! Ocean of Mercy! You seem to have come here for performing *tapas*, and yet you shower grace upon your devotees. O Adorable Goddess, but for a play of *maya* how can the universe come into existence! It is impossible for anyone to comprehend or describe fully your *maya*.' Saying this the old sage welcomed Ambika.

With humility and respect he offered Her a seat woven of sacred grass and water for washing Her feet. After completing the worship he took a seat at the bidding of the Goddess. With devotion and bliss overflowing and his voice choking with emotion, the Sage addressed the Goddess:

Ah! This can surely only be the outcome of Sambhu's boundless grace. He who loves His devotees has sent you here with the object of protecting them. O Mother! Is there anything wanting or not attained after seeing you? Bhagavati! Be so gracious as to command me, Thy servant, as to what I can do for you.

# V. Gautama Narrates the Glory of Arunachala

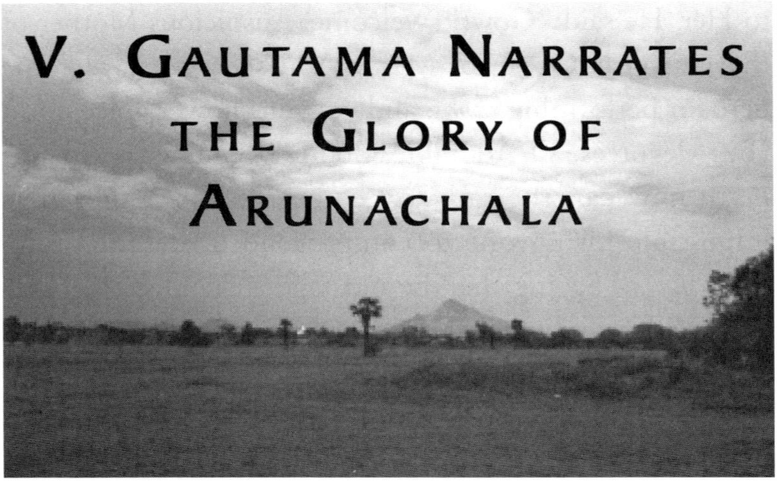

On hearing the words of the all-knowing Maharshi, Ambika praised him and said graciously:

It is because your glory is so great that Siva, the Lord of the *devas*, commanded me to meet you. You alone have reached the other shore of the *Agamas* and the Vedas. By your austerities you alone among the devotees of Siva have become very dear to Him. My Lord told me that He abides here as Arunachala, and directed me to learn its glory from you. I have therefore come to practise austerities in the vicinity of Arunachala. By merely seeking you, one will obtain the Grace of the Lord. The object of taking birth in this world is companionship with the devotees of Siva, listening to His praise and worshipping Him in all His forms. I look upon you as my father for you are the personification of wisdom. Therefore, pray, kindly enlighten me on the glory of Arunachala. On hearing Gowri speak thus, Gautama, the repository of austerities, meditated upon the Lord for sometime and addressed the Goddess:

Gowri, you are the embodiment of universal knowledge and represent Siva's divine illusion as *maya*. What have I got to say about the glory of Arunachala that you are not already aware of! Probably, you love to hear from the lips of devotees about the greatness of your Lord! To speak of the greatness of Siva is as auspicious as the study and recital of the Vedas. My austerities have borne fruit only now. By the grace of Hara and Gowri I am now going to describe the Effulgent glory of Arunachala. This ancient, sacred lore shall be listened to with faith, devotion and in rapt attention by generations to come and shall be known as the glory of Arunachala!

Even a million tongues cannot delineate fully how the formless, Supreme Being out of compassion took this holy form of Arunachala Hill. Nay, even if a million Brahmas came together, they would fail to narrate His glory satisfactorily. Arunachala in this form was in former times worshipped by Brahma, Vishnu, Soma (the moon), Surya (the sun), Agni (fire), Indra and the other *devas*, *dikpalakas* (the protectors of the quarters), *siddhas*, *charanas*, *yakshas*, *vidyadharas*, *gandharvas*, *nagas*, serpents, birds, divine sages, *siddha yogis* and others, in order to get rid of their sins and to obtain the fulfilment of their desires.

The Lord of Arunagiri is capable of removing all the sins of those who merely see Him and of fulfilling all the desires of those who worship Him. He is capable of granting

Liberation even to those who utter the word 'Arunachala' from a distance. It is well known that what is called 'Arunadri' is the embodiment of Effulgence. *Yogis* meditate upon it and attain union with Siva. Offerings, sacrifices, and *japa* made in its vicinity yield immeasurable results.

In olden times, Brahma and Vishnu who had come into existence from a tiny part of the Effulgence of Siva, became egoistic, and wishing to assert their supremacy fought with each other. Sadasiva, in order to destroy their pride, appeared in their midst as a blazing Column of Fire without beginning, middle or end illumining the entire cosmos. They desired to ascertain what It was. So they assumed the forms of a swan and a boar and proceeded towards the sky and the nether regions respectively. Seeing them tired and distressed at being unable to find either beginning or end of the Column of Fire, Bhagavan, the embodiment of compassion, took pity on His children and emerged from the brilliant Column with the intention of blessing them and granting the boons desired by them. Their pride now stood completely annihilated. At their request Siva took the form of a motionless hill known as *Arunadri* and also consented to abide there eternally in the form of a *linga*, so that they and other devotees could worship Him as prescribed in the *Agamas*. This Effulgent *Linga*, in the form of a hill was duly worshipped by the previous ninety-six Brahmas, creators of the worlds.[1]

---

[1] According to Hindu scriptures, after each dissolution of the universe the creator Brahma merges with Sadasiva and the next in lineage becomes the creator. Thus what Gautama means is that already ninety-six dissolutions had taken place. This coincides with geological findings which put the core age of Arunachala as 3.8 billion years.

Gautama further related how Tilothama, the celestial damsel, was saved from the amorous advances of Brahma who in his lust wanted to covet her. When she sought refuge at the feet of Arunachala, the Lord saved her and chastised Brahma. Brahma implored Siva for forgiveness. The Lord on His part bestowed His Grace on Brahma and said: 'The time which has already been allotted to you by me will not undergo any change. Not even the greatest are free from the evils of desire. Therefore, meditate upon the Effulgent *Linga* known as Arunachala and be rid of all your sins. All the evil produced by mind, speech and body shall be destroyed the moment one beholds Arunachala. This Arunagiri will cleanse all the sins of those who circumambulate it, prostrate to it, remember it and offer flowers, or praise it with devotion. While mountains like Kailasa and Meru are my places of abode, this Arunagiri is my true form and here I abide eternally as this Hill. By merely looking at its peak not only will all sins be destroyed but the eye of wisdom will be opened.

'Once upon a time one of the Brahmas who had come into existence from a tiny part of my person bathed in the *Pushkarini* (sacred pool) bearing his name and got rid of his delusion. You who are in the form of the world, may also, after bathing in the *Brahma Tirtha*[2] and after offering flowers to me, silently go round the hill, get rid of your sins and be blessed.'

On hearing this, Brahma bathed in the pool and worshipped Mahesa who stood in the form of a mountain.

[2] This *Brahma Tirtha* can be seen inside the great temple of Arunachaleswara.

This Brahma worshipped Arunagiri with great devotion, with a mind made pure by control (*yama-niyama*), got rid of his sins and became the lord of the world.

Gautama continued:

Once Lord Narayana, the protector of the universe, having the thousand-tongued serpent Adisesha (representing intellect and knowledge) as his couch, was reclining in the ocean of milk *(kshirasagara)*, absorbed in *yoga-nidra* and oblivious to the dissolution of the universe. The whole cosmic space was enveloped in complete darkness. The sages were worried over this state of affairs. They prayed to Lord Siva. The Lord manifested Himself before them with the object of protecting the universe. From the Effulgent Sambhu, thirty-three crore *devas* emerged as sparks and scattered in all directions. These *devas* went to Vishnu and informed him of what had happened. He pondered: Overcome by darkness (ignorance) I fell into an untimely sleep, forgetting my real nature. Sadasiva, the supremely Effulgent Being, seems to have revealed His form in order to wake me up and taken upon Himself the task of creating the worlds. What remains for me or Brahma to do?

Then meditating on Sadasiva, Vishnu prostrated before Him and repeatedly saluted Him. Thus he absolved himself of his omissions. Whereupon, the protector of those who seek refuge in Him, blessed Vishnu with compassion and bade him rise. Vishnu then stood up and prayed thus:

Lord of the three worlds! Thou who once destroyed the three cities of the demons by Thy laughter! According to the law of cause and effect, through the crores of *devas* Thou performest deeds by Thy will alone. Out of ignorance I fell into *yoga-nidra*, O Sambhu! Kindly forgive my sin! When Hara (Siva) heard Hari (Vishnu) lamenting in this manner He prescribed the following penance for Vishnu:

I abide on earth in the form of Arunachala. The moment you set your eyes on it your ignorance will be destroyed. On a previous occasion I gave a boon to another Vishnu at that place. My manifestation at that time was known as the Effulgent *Linga* of Arunachala. That Effulgent *Linga* has cooled down for the sake of the world. Nevertheless, it is fiery, unmanifest and of untold glory. Since its Effulgence is latent, streams, rivers and rainwater are absorbed by it. Moreover its glory gives sight to the blind, ability to walk to the lame, progeny to the childless, and speech to the dumb. Arunachala confers all *siddhis*, cures all diseases, destroys all sins and grants all boons.

After declaring thus Mahadeva (Siva) disappeared and Vishnu came to Arunachala. He practised austerities and worshipped Arunachala. He visited the *devas* living in the forests around the Hill and built holy *ashrams* for the sages. He recreated the Vedas, *Vedangas* and *Upanishads*, etc. He bathed in the *Brahma Tirtha*, circumambulated Arunachala, got rid of his sins and attained the lordship of all the worlds.

Surya (Sun) the lord of all the planets, in an attempt to cross over Arunachala, lost his splendour and could not proceed on his heavenly orbit. He then, on the advice of

Brahma, worshipped Arunachala, whereupon he regained his strength by His grace and was able to proceed on his course. Since then, Surya does not pass over the Red Hill; he goes around it.

Further, the Sun who was harassed by the *asuras* (demons) devoutly worshipped the Lord of Arunachala. He bathed in the holy *Brahma Tirtha* and circumambulated Arunachala. Thereby he conquered all the *asuras* and gained the ability to circumambulate Mount Meru. He also acquired the power to outshine all other celestial luminaries.

Chandra (Moon) who was harassed by the curse of Daksha Prajapati, worshipped Arunachala as advised by Siva Himself and regained his original form. Agni (Fire) although tainted by the disease of consumption under the curse of a *Brahmarishi*, was cured by worshipping Arunachala.

Indra had incurred sin by slaying Vritra, Bala, Paka, Namuchi and Jrimbha who had in ancient times obtained boons from Siva and had become lords of the worlds. He lost his vigour and his kingdom. As directed by Siva, he worshipped Arunachala in the prescribed manner and got rid of his sin. Afterwards he performed *Aswamedha yaga* and pleasing Siva thereby, regained his status as lord of *devas*.

The serpent Adisesha worshipped the Lord of the Red Hill and acquired, by Siva's Grace, the strength to bear the earth. The other serpents as well as the *gandharvas*, *siddhas, apsaras* and *dikpalakas* obtained the boons they desired by worshipping the Hill. The *devas* who wished to conquer the *asuras* paid their obeisance to Arunachala and obtained His grace.

In ancient days the *devas* who lost their limbs at the sacrifice of Daksha gained new limbs by the grace of Arunachala.

Sukra, Aruna, a king named Pratardana, a *gandharva* named Pushpaka and many others expiated their sins and regained their original forms by worshipping Arunachala. Such is His glory!

The land within a radius of three *yojanas* (approximately thirty miles) of this place is famous as *Sivabhumi* (the land of Siva). Those who reside within this limit will certainly attain Liberation. In olden days the 'Seven Rishis' who were under a spell, worshipped Arunachala regarding Him as their Lord. The Lord of Arunachala thereupon redeemed them. Grateful, they dug a tank near the Hill, bathing in which all sins are removed.

A sage who was lame, came to Arunachala hoping to regain his legs. Praying mentally, with crutches in hand and knees worn out, he proceeded to the bank of the river Sona to quench his thirst. Having left his crutches on the bank he began to drink the water. At that time someone pretending to be quenching his thirst first threw the crutches into the water and then asked him angrily, "How dare you come to Arunachala with crutches? Why do you need them?" then he disappeared. The lame man at once regained the use of his legs. With folded hands he saluted Arunachala and proceeded towards his house. Other noble devotees of Siva marvelled at this miracle and saluted the lame sage who had regained his limbs.[3]

Vali, the son of Indra, once tried to pass over Arunagiri while travelling from Udayagiri (the hill of sunrise) to Astamanagiri (the hill of sunset) but lost his strength and fell down to earth. Then Indra, his father, came and told him that this was no ordinary Hill and extolled the greatness of Arunachala. Upon this, Vali worshipped the *Linga* of Effulgence and regained his strength.

Nala, who was the personification of *dharma*, worshipped this Hill and ruled his kingdom in a just manner. He was transformed into a woman for entering the garden of Gowri. Not knowing why this had happened to him, he asked his preceptor (*guru*) and, on his advice, worshipped Arunachala. He regained his original masculine

---

[3] There is a similar incident which took place at the beginning of the twentieth century. It has been recorded by Devaraja Mudaliar in his *My Recollections of Bhagavan Ramana:*

There was an elderly cripple who was a very devout man and who used to circumambulate Arunachala in spite of his disability. After many years' at Tiruvannamalai, he once got so vexed at the treatment he received from the relatives with whom he was staying and on whom he depended, that he decided in disgust to leave Tiruvannamalai and go away to some village and try to earn a living there. Before he left the outskirts of the town, a young *Brahmin* appeared before him and, with apparent rudeness, snatched away his crutches, saying "You don't deserve these". Before the old man's indignation could get the better of him, he found he had recovered the use of his limbs and could walk without crutches.

Bhagavan said he knew this case personally, remarking on its similarity to the case mentioned in *Arunachala Sthala Purana.* Bhagavan said that he knew that these things took place, but did not say who did them or how they happened. Some of his earlier devotees have told me it was really Bhagavan who was responsible for such miracles, and I am inclined to agree.

form. Soma, advised to think of Arunagiri always, did so, and obtaining by the strength of his austerities, the Lord's grace, got rid of his curse and also attained a state unattainable even by the immortals (*amaras*). Hari felt great sorrow on account of his separation from his consort. But, on the advice of the sage Bhrigu, he worshipped Arunagiri and got over his sorrows in all his incarnations. Saraswati, Savitri, Sri Devi, Bhoo Devi and other goddesses and the rivers were blessed and attained immortality by the Grace of Lord Arunachala.

Surya abides under the protection of Arunachala in the east, Visvamitra in the south, Varuna in the west and Trisuladeva (the Lord of the trident) in the north. These four gods dwell on the hills which are at a distance of two *yojanas* and do obeisance to Arunachala. The gods who dwell in the four corners of Arunachala bow down to Siva who abides in the form of Arunachala.

On the northern peak of Arunachala there is a giant banyan tree. Maheswara sits beneath it in the guise of a *siddha*. Its shade extends to a long distance around it. Even the gods look upon it in wonder. This Hill shines with eight *lingas* placed in the eight quarters, and is worshipped by the protectors of the respective quarters. There is a wish-fulfilling *bakula* tree at this place. The Sage Vamadeva is reputed to be performing meditation under it. Agastya and Vasishta worshipped the Lord of Aruna. In ancient days Sonanada, the son of Hiranyagarbha, performed severe austerities and made the Ganga appear here. That holy river now flows here as the

Sona river. The sacred river named Vena flows round the Hill. Bhagavan Marut bathed in the holy tank of Vayu in the quarter belonging to Vayu, and became the life-breath (*prana*) of the world.

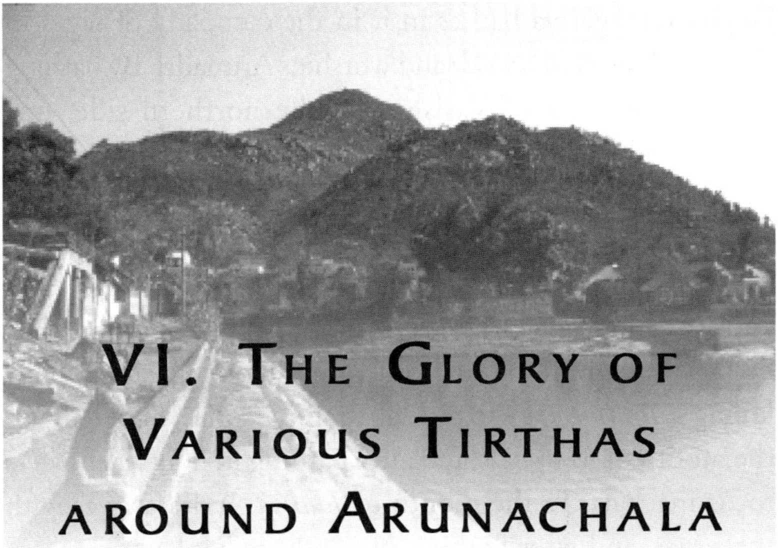

# VI. The Glory of Various Tirthas around Arunachala

ON the northern side of the Hill is situated the holy tank of Kubera containing lotuses of sweet fragrance. In the quarter belonging to Isanya (north-east) lies the holy tank of Isanya. The lotus-eyed Vishnu bathed in the holy tank on the western side. The nine planets acquired their status as a result of bathing in it. Those who bathe in that holy tank obtain the blessings of the nine planets. Durga, Vinayaka, Skanda, Kshetrapala, Saraswati, other gods and goddesses dwell round the holy tank of Brahma and protect it. The Ganga, the Yamuna, the Godavari, the Saraswati, the Narmada, the Sindhu, the Kaveri, the Sonanada and the Sona rivers are reputed to flow unseen around Arunachala.

It is said that by bathing in the holy tank of Agastya on the southern side, one acquires a knowledge of several languages. Agastya bathes in it in the company of sages in the month of *Bhadrapada* and worships Arunadri. By bathing in the holy tank of Vasishta on the northern side, one understands the meaning of the Vedas. Vasishta comes here from Mount Meru in the month of *Asvija* and, after bathing in it, meditates upon the Lord of Sona. In the month of *Kartika*, the Ganga and other holy waters arrive here together and worship Arunadri with devotion. By worshipping the holy tank of Brahma in front of Arunadri, great sins like killing a *Brahmin* are expiated. Brahma comes here daily in the month of *Margazhi* and after bathing in it, offers flowers to Arunachala. In the month of *Pushya*, Indra arrives with the *devas*, and after bathing in it salutes Sankara.

There is also a great *tirtha* named *Saivam* in front of Arunachala. Rudra bathes in it holding in his hand the *Brahmakapala* (the skull of Brahma). Sambhu graciously dwells in it in the company of his followers in the month of *Magha*, and thereby absolves people of their sins. Agni bathed in the auspicious *Agni Tirtha* situated in the quarter of Agni (south-east) and obtained Goddess Svaha for his consort. Kama, the god of love, bathed in it in the month of *Phalguni*, and by worshipping Sonadri, became the lord of all pleasures. *Brahmarishis* always dwell joyfully at the *Vaishnavateertha* (sacred tank of Vishnu) on the south-east. Vishnu goes there in the month of *Chitra*, and after bathing in it, meditates upon the Lord of Arunadri. It is by doing so that he became the Lord of all the worlds.

The *Surya Tirtha* (sacred tank of Surya, the Sun) situated in the quarter of Kubera (north), is capable of curing all diseases. Bhagavan Surya comes there in the month of *Vaikasi* and after bathing in it, adores the Lord. The *Asvini devas* bathed in the pure *Asvini Tirtha* (sacred tank of the *Asvins*), situated in the quarter of *Isa Brahma Uttara* (north-east), and became pure. The *Pandava Tirtha* (sacred tank of the Pandavas) situated at the foot of Arunachala is well known for its auspicious qualities, and is capable of fulfilling desires and bestowing Liberation. The Pandavas bathed in it and became the lords of the world. Bhoo Devi (Goddess Earth) was blessed with all herbs and fruits as a result of bathing in it along with all the *devas* in the month of *Jyeshta*.

The *Vaisvadeva Tirtha* (sacred tank of the *Visvedevas*) situated in the quarter of *Soma Surya Uttara* (north-west), is famous for bestowing lordship of the world. The *Visvedevas*, although very powerful, could not obtain their share of sacrifices. They therefore bathed in it in the month of *Ashada*, adored Siva, and thereby overcame their disability. By bathing in the famous *Indra Tirtha* (sacred water of Indra) situated in the east, Goddess Lakshmi was wedded to Lord Vishnu. By bathing in the *Skanda Tirtha* on the north, Skanda became very powerful. Agastya Kumbhaka and Kumbha always dwell in the *Kumbha Tirtha* on the west, famous for its holiness. The Ganga worships Arunachala at its feet, the Yamuna in the middle and the Narmada at the top.

There are many other *tirthas* also. Even Sage Markandeya did not know all of them. That king of sages pleased the Lord by his austerities, and lovingly begged for the following boon: Bhagavan Arunadri! There are thousands of *tirthas*. They will not be visible to persons of meagre knowledge. How can men find them all in one place? It is not possible for a man to worship them one by one. You must withdraw all your Effulgence within yourself and manifest as Sonadri worshipped by all the *devas* who are afraid of approaching you.

Gautama continued:

I too by the Grace of Siva adored Him in the form of Arunachala and worshipped the invisible *Linga* for the benefit of the entire world. A celestial pavilion was constructed here by Visvakarma. Various festivals and celebrations were introduced. Sages found several kinds of scriptures dealing with *dharma* and conducted the worship of Siva in accordance with them.

I also appointed seven noble maidens sprung from the sacrificial fire, for the worship of Siva. In olden days the Lord of Sonasaila was specially worshipped by many kings who had regained their kingdoms after conquering their enemies.

This *Linga* in the form of a hill is blemishless and is named Annamalai. The Lord of Arunagiri, who grants boons, should always be meditated upon. Fortunate indeed are the noble souls who have acquired boundless merit by worshipping the Lord of Arunachala who protects his devotees and absolves them of sins the moment they think of Him. May you too meditate upon Him and achieve your object.

# VII. The Glory of Various Tirthas

PARVATI enquired: How did this *Linga* of fire come to exist on earth? How did it become cool and easily visible to all beings? How are the holy waters rising from this sacred hill withdrawn into it? You must enlighten me.

Gautama said: This hill was a mass of fire in the *Krita Yuga*, jewels in the *Treta Yuga*, gold in the *Dvapara Yuga* and emerald in the *Kali Yuga*. In the *Krita Yuga*, when it spread out for several *yojanas* as a mass of fire, Maharshis circumambulated it. Thereafter, at the humble prayer of the *devas*, Bhagavan Arunachala gradually became cool.

Gautama continued: The *devas* prayed thus: 'Bhagavan! Lord of Arunagiri! Although your nature is fiery you must illuminate the world in a cool form. The Vedas regard you as the embodiment of Siva and proclaim you as "that which is copper-coloured, bright, crimson red and wholly auspicious". Salutations to you who are known by the Vedas and who are Soma and pure bliss. The whole world, moving and un- moving, is your form. Therefore it is your form that is seen as *devas*. You produce at the end of *yugas*, cloudbursts, flooded streams and overflowing oceans. For it is said in the Vedas: "From fire, water came into existence." It is therefore said that the world came into existence from you who are the Supreme Self. O Mahadeva! Sonachala! Ocean of Compassion! O Lord! Let all men know you.'

When the *devas* humbly prayed, the Lord who loves His devotees immediately became cool and visible to all. Thereafter rivers and streams began to flow. Rains falling from the clouds were no longer withdrawn into the hill. An Effulgence bright as millions of rising suns can be seen in the eyes of enlightened *jivas* who worship it. In accordance with the prayers of the *dikpalakas*, *devas*, *maharshis* and other great souls, all the *tirthas* wander around the Hill.

Brahma said: On hearing these details, Gowri enquired with great enthusiasm about the true origin of the *tirthas*. She asked: 'O Bhagavan! Which of the *tirthas* here are invisible and which are visible? Please tell me!' Gautama recollected what Siva had formerly told him and said: The *Indra Tirtha* is situated in the east; Indra got rid of the sin of killing a Brahmin by bathing in it. The *Brahma Tirtha* is situated in the quarter of Agni (southeast); Agni's sin of seducing the wives of others was removed by bathing in it. On the south is the *Yama Tirtha*; Yama was saved from the fear of *Brahmastra* (a divine weapon) by bathing in it. On the southwest is the *Nairta Tirtha*; The *rishis* conquered the *bhutas* and *vetalas* by bathing in it. On the west is *Varuna Tirtha*; Varuna obtained an ever-full quiver by bathing in it. On the northwest is the *Vayu Tirtha*; Vayu attained the power of becoming the life-breath of the world by bathing in it. On the north is the *Soma Tirtha*; Chandra (moon) was cured of consumption by bathing in it. On the northeast is the *Isana Tirtha*; Vishnu attained Goddess Sri for his wife by bathing in it.

In olden days, Markandeya bowed down to Isvara and prayed: Sadasiva! Mahadeva! Deva of *devas*! Lord of the world! Sankara Bhagavan! You must tell me the means of bringing together at this place all the various *tirthas*. On hearing this the Lord of Uma was greatly pleased and described to him the means: All the *tirthas* abide unseen in my presence at the time of my worship and adore me. Great sage! You need not go anywhere seeking *tirthas*. At the time of my worship all the *tirthas* come together to this place. Therefore devotees, all sages and *devas* may see the congregation of all *tirthas* here immediately after *naivedya* is offered to me.

Goddess! In olden days Siva described to Markandeya the means of seeing all the *tirthas*. All the sacred *tirthas* are visible in front of Siva at the time of worship.

On hearing the words of the Sage, the daughter of the king of the mountains was pleased and said: The goal of my life has been attained by me, by duly learning from you the means of worshipping the wonderful *tirthas* on earth. O glorious performer of austerities! The benefit of all the *tirthas* has been obtained. I thank you. Siva Himself has commanded me to do penance here. How shall men worship on earth the Supreme Lord Parameswara who, although really terribly fiery, is also cool in the form of a Hill?

# VIII. Worship of Arunachala

GAUTAMA said: Goddess! Hear what happened long ago. At Sankara's command I visited places sacred to Him, such as Kedar, Badarikasrama, Kasi, Sri Parvata, Kancheepuram, Tiruchuzhi etc. I worshipped the *lingas* installed by sages and great *yogis* and bathed in the *tirthas*. I practised austerities along with my disciples and performed *yajnas* (sacrifices). Finally I had *darshan* of Arunadri, the *Linga* in the form of the famous Hill Arunachala. Here, I saw *tapasvins* who were engrossed in penance and worshipping Sonagiri, subsisting upon roots. Seeing their devotion I too fell in love with this great *Linga* and with great fervour began to adore Arunachala which had first been worshipped by Brahma. I prayed: Lord of Arunachala that art acclaimed by the Vedas in the words, *Asau yastamra aruna uta bhabhru sumangalah*. Siva!

The Supreme Self! Thou that art the embodiment of Vedas! Eternal One! Slayer of the God of time (*Kala-Kala*)! Beloved of Thy devotees! Destroyer of the Three Cities! Lord of the *devas*! By merely looking at Thee one obtains the merit that accrues by following all the *dharmas*. One need not practise austerities thereafter. Even the *devas* wish to dwell in this abode of Thine. Time being now propitious for me, I have the good fortune of dwelling here. The austerities practised by me have enabled me to see Thee. Thy form is awe-inspiring. Nowhere else in the world can one see a *linga* in the form of a hill. This form constitutes the three gods, Brahma, Vishnu and Siva. It controls the three phases of time as well as the three kinds of powers (*saktis*). This wonderful *Linga* is the essence of the three Vedas. Thou abidest on earth in this form as the famous Sonadri (Red Hill) for protecting the three worlds. In front of me I see that form, most auspicious, most compassionate and the refuge of all *jivas*. Pray, save me.

Sonachala, whom I praised in this manner, revealed thereupon His divine form to me, called me to His side and, after listening to the praises sung with such great devotion, said: I am greatly pleased with you. You shall worship me according to ancient custom and perform austerities and thus proclaim my glory to all. When you were practising austerities on the Kailasa Mountain I ordered you to come to the southern country and worship Arunachala. The *Saptarishis* worship me on earth in the same way and do good to all living beings through the power of their austerities. Worship me in accordance with the method laid down in the *agamas*. This glorious and divine method of worshipping me is worthy of being seen even by the *devas* of *swarga*. Make it clear to all that Arunachala in this physical form, composed of earth, is truly Siva. There are ever so many virtuous souls who, having formerly worshipped me, are now living on earth in great joy. As you are superior to all of them you must clearly expound the proper method of worshipping Siva.

On being commanded thus by the Lord, I bowed down to Him and reverently asked Him: How can I worship the Lord who is fiery and unapproachable? How am I to carry out Thy command? Kindly tell me how I am to understand Thy words. The Lord of Arunachala then replied as follows: I shall describe to you the *lingas* on earth which are in their subtle form. You may worship me in accordance with the *agamas* and with the power of your austerities.

Saying this, Swayambhu revealed Himself to me as Siva. On seeing this *Linga* adorned with all kinds of ornaments, I felt that the goal of my life had been attained. I again begged Siva who is fond of His devotees, thus: How can name and form be attributed to Thee who cannot be described even by the *agamas*? Who can worship Thee with flowers? Where is the temple for Thee? Or how is one to be built? Which is the hymn to praise Thee? In what manner art Thou to be worshipped? Who is Thy bodyguard? How is one to make people believe that ever so many celestial beings (*devatas*) always abide in Thy presence? Supreme Lord! Thou must kindly explain all this to me.

When I prayed thus, the Lord ordered Visvakarma as follows: You must create here a divine and noble city named Arunachala. You must also build in it a divine temple adorned with jewels. Arrangements should be made in the temple for chanting the Vedas, and for singing, dancing and playing musical instruments as part of my worship.

The peerless Sambhu then explained to me the proper order of chanting His different names while offering flowers and the rules prescribed for it. He said: Gautama! I shall describe how mortals should worship me. Listen. Know also who are the persons to be appointed for my worship. You must worship Arunachala which appears as a lustrous and immeasurable *Linga* on earth, for the welfare of the entire world. Let my power (*sakti*) which is inseparable from me and sustains the glory of this temple be installed on my northern side and worshipped as Apitakuchambika. The Lord of Arunachala is fond of Her and never parts from Her. Let offerings be duly made to Him. Let Sundareswari be worshipped during auspicious festivals. Since Bala Ganapati is the bestower of all prosperity, let Him be well adorned and worshipped in front of Me. Nataraja who is fond of dancing, Amritesvara and Parasakti should also be worshipped. Let the goddesses who remove obstacles be installed on the southern side, and Skanda who carries the weapon known as Sakti, on the north-east.

I should be worshipped in the innermost shrine (*mulasthana*), Dakshinamurti in the south, Maha Vishnu in the form of Agni in the West, Brahma in the East and in a separate shrine on the northern side, Goddess Unnamulai should be well adorned, accompanied by all the *devas* and surrounded by the *dikpalakas*. The extremely glorious *devis,* the fully adorned *Kshetrapalaka* (the protector of the temple), *devatas* who maintain the traditions, should all be worshipped for ensuring the prosperity of the temple. Monthly festivals should be grandly celebrated. Let *dikshitars* who are learned in the Vedas, virtuous, prosperous, pure in heart and well-versed in the *agamas* of Siva, be appointed for rendering divine service. Let highly accomplished persons be engaged to play on musical instruments at the time of worship. Let *pandits* learned in *Sadvidya* and *Chaturvidya* and *kshatriyas, vaisyas* and others who are devotees of Siva be encouraged to settle here. Let *mutts* be constructed on all four sides for the accommodation of pilgrims and the residence of ascetics, sages and devotees of Siva. Let *pasupatas* (a sect among *Saivites*), *kapalikas* (another sect who use *kapala,* 'human skull' in their rituals) and *Sivayogis* live in these *mutts,* beg their food and worship Siva. The kings should protect this place without violating my commands.

There is a *makizha* (*bakula*) tree at this place. All temple affairs should be decided under it. Money offered to the temple will yield boundless merit. I listen to the prayers of devotees at that spot and grant the boons desired by them. I pardon all the faults of those who adore me.

I accept the worship conducted by mortals as laid down in the *agamas*. Pious acts performed by my devotees please Me. O Sage! You must examine the *agamas* and prescribe the methods of worshipping Me. Let special *pujas* be conducted on full-moon days. Let thousands of *sattras* (inns) supply free food on that day. Let everyone make gifts according to his ability. There is no doubt that those who keep a light burning continuously before me, will become Effulgent Beings like me.

Having heard these words of Sambhu my doubts were cleared. I bowed to the Lord of Arunagiri and prayed to Him.

Gautama said to Siva: I wish to learn from Thee Thy names which are to be used during worship in this temple.

Thereupon the Lord said: O Sage! Listen to my names which fulfil all desires:

The names of Siva (Arunachala):

| | | | |
|---|---|---|---|
| 1 | *Sonadrisah* | .. | Lord of the Red Hill |
| 2 | *Arunadrisah* | .. | Lord of the Crimson Hill |
| 3 | *Devadhisah* | .. | Lord of *devas* |
| 4 | *Janapriyah* | .. | Beloved of people |
| 5 | *Prapannarakshakah* | .. | Protector of those who seek refuge with Him |
| 6 | *Dhirah* | .. | Brave One |
| 7 | *Sivah* | .. | The auspicious One |
| 8 | *Sevakavartakah* | .. | He who is devoted to His votaries |
| 9 | *Amrtesanah* | .. | Lord of the nectar |
| 10 | *Stripumbhava-pradayakah* | .. | Granter of birth as man or woman |

| | | | |
|---|---|---|---|
| 11 | *Bhaktavijnapti-samadhata* | .. | He who answers the prayers of His devotees |
| 12 | *Dinabandha-vimochakah* | .. | He who releases the lowly from bondage |
| 13 | *Mukharanghripatih* | .. | He from whose footfall sound originates |
| 14 | *Sriman* | .. | The noble One |
| 15 | *Mrdah* | .. | He whose form is Bliss |
| 16 | *Mrgamadesvarah* | .. | He who is fond of musk |
| 17 | *Bhaktaprekshanakrit* | .. | He who makes His devotees His messengers |
| 18 | *Sakshi* | .. | The Witness |
| 19 | *Bhaktadoshanivartakah.* | .. | He who removes the delusion of His devotees |
| 20 | *Sangitavetta* | .. | He who is expert in music |
| 21 | *Nrittajnah* | .. | He who is proficient in the art of dancing |
| 22 | *Trivedi* | .. | Lord of the three Vedas |
| 23 | *Vrddhavaidikah* | .. | The Ancient One of the Vedas |
| 24 | *Tyagarajah* | .. | The Ocean of Compassion |
| 25 | *Krpasindhuh* | .. | The merciful one |
| 26 | *Sugandhi* | .. | The sweet-scented One |
| 27 | *Sourabhesvarah* | .. | The Lord of the Bull |
| 28 | *Kartaviryesvarah* | .. | The Lord of Kartavirya |
| 29 | *Santah* | .. | The Peaceful One |

| | | | |
|---|---|---|---|
| 30 | *Kapali* | .. | The wearer of skulls |
| 31 | *Kalasaprabhuh* | .. | The Lord of the ceremonial pitcher in which all gods are worshipped |
| 32 | *Jnanasambandhanatah* | .. | Lord of Jnanasambandha |
| 33 | *Sri Halahalasundarah* | .. | The Lord who consumed the deadly poison |
| 34 | *Ahvaisvaryadata* | .. | He who confers prosperity spontaneously |
| 35 | *Smartrsarvaghanasanah* | .. | He who removes the impurities of those who think of Him |
| 36 | *Vyatyastanrityah* | .. | He who raised the left foot in dancing |
| 37 | *Dhwajadhrk* | .. | Bearer of the banner |
| 38 | *Sakantih* | .. | The bright One |
| 39 | *Natesah* | .. | Lord of dancing |
| 40 | *Samapriyah* | .. | Lover of the Sama Veda |
| 41 | *Papaharah* | .. | Destroyer of sin |
| 42 | *Vedamurtih* | .. | Embodiment of the Vedas |
| 43 | *Niranjanah* | .. | The taintless One |
| 44 | *Jagannathah* | .. | Lord of the world |
| 45 | *Mahadevah* | .. | The Great God |
| 46 | *Trinetrah* | .. | The three-eyed God |

| | | | |
|---|---|---|---|
| 47 | *Tripurantakah* | .. | Destroyer of the three cities |
| 48 | *Bhaktaparadhasoda* | .. | He who pardons the faults of His devotees |
| 49 | *Yogisah* | .. | King of *yogis* |
| 50 | *Bhoganayakah* | .. | Lord of enjoyments |
| 51 | *Kalamurtih* | .. | Embodiment of Time |
| 52 | *Kshamarupi* | .. | Embodiment of forgiveness |
| 53 | *Dharmarakshakah* | .. | Protector of *Dharma* |
| 54 | *Vrshadhwajah* | .. | He whose banner bears the emblem of the Bull |
| 55 | *Harah* | .. | The Destroyer |
| 56 | *Girisvarah* | .. | Lord of the Hill |
| 57 | *Chandrarekhavatamsakah.* | . | The wearer of the Crescent Moon |
| 58 | *Smarantakah* | .. | The foe of Kama(Cupid) |
| 59 | *Andhakaripuh* | .. | The destroyer of the demon Andhaka |
| 60 | *Siddharajah* | .. | The All-powerful One |
| 61 | *Digambarah* | .. | He for whom the quarters are clothes |
| 62 | *Isanah* | .. | The Originator |
| 63 | *Devadevah* | .. | Deva of *devas* |
| 64 | *Bhasmarudraksha-lanchanah* | .. | The wearer of the sacred ash and *rudraksha* beads |
| 65 | *Sripatih* | .. | Lord of wealth |

| | | | |
|---|---|---|---|
| 66 | *Sankarah* | .. | The Gracious One |
| 67 | *Srashta* | .. | The Creator |
| 68 | *Sarvavoidyesvarah* | .. | He who is well-versed in the arts |
| 69 | *Anaghah* | .. | He who is faultless |
| 70 | *Gangadharah* | .. | The wearer of the Ganga |
| 71 | *Kratudhvamsi* | .. | Destroyer of the sacrifice |
| 72 | *Vimalah* | .. | He who is without blemish |
| 73 | *Nagabhushanah* | .. | Wearer of the serpent |
| 74 | *Arunah* | .. | He who is fiery and therefore without form |
| 75 | *Bahurupah* | .. | He who has many forms |
| 76 | *Virupakshah* | .. | The possessor of the Infinite Eye |
| 77 | *Aksharakrtih* | .. | He whose form is *Akshara* |
| 78 | *Anadirantarahitah* | .. | He who has no beginning or end |
| 79 | *Sivakamah* | .. | He who desires the welfare of all |
| 80 | *Swayamprabhuh* | .. | He who is His own chief |
| 81 | *Satchidanandarupah* | .. | He whose form is Being-Consciousness-Bliss |
| 82 | *Sarvatma* | .. | The Self of all |
| 83 | *Jivadharakah* | .. | The supporter of all |

| | | | |
|---|---|---|---|
| 84 | *Strisangavamasubhagah.* | .. | He from whom emanates *Sakti* (Power) and who is the most beautiful One |
| 85 | *Vihitasundarah* | .. | The One who is beautiful when taken out in procession |
| 86 | *Jnanapradah* | .. | The Teacher of Wisdom |
| 87 | *Muktidah* | .. | The bestower Liberation |
| 88 | *Bhaktavanchitadayakah.* | .. | Granter of devotees' prayers |
| 89 | *Ascharyavaibhavah* | .. | The possessor of wonderful glory |
| 90 | *Kami* | .. | He who is full of love |
| 91 | *Niravadhyah* | .. | He who is free from evil |
| 92 | *Nidhipradah* | .. | The bestower of wealth |
| 93 | *Sarvanami* | .. | The possessor of all names |
| 94 | *Manovasah* | .. | The dweller in the mind |
| 95 | *Sarvah* | .. | The Lord of all |
| 96 | *Arunagirisvarah* | .. | The Lord of Arunagiri |

These are my principal names. Remember also the divine names mentioned in the *puranas*. Worship me everyday with these names and as prescribed in the *Agamas*.

# IX. The Glory of Circumambulating Arunachala

WORSHIP me especially by circumambulating me everyday. For I, the Lord of Sonachala am pleased when devotees circumambulate me.

Gautama continued: As the Lord commanded I always live here and worship Arunachala.

Upon this Gowri asked the Sage: Knower of all *dharmas*! Gautama! Kindly describe to me the glory of circumambulating Arunachala. When is it to be done and how? Who are they who have till now circumambulated it and attained their objects? Who has attained the supreme state by doing so?

Gautama replied: 'Goddess! Hear what the great Siva told me. He said: While I abide gloriously on earth as Arunachala all the *devatas* and *munis* circumambulate Me. At every step that one takes on the path round Me all the sins committed in one's past lives are expiated. By circumambulating Me one obtains the merit of performing thousands of horse sacrifices, innumerable *Vajapeyas* (a particular sacrifice) and bathing in all the *tirthas*. Even a great sinner who has no good deed to his credit can attain all kinds of powers by circumambulating Me. Merit acquired by bathing in all the *tirthas*, by performing all the sacrifices, by studying all the scriptures and by following all the *dharmas* can be easily acquired by merely circumambulating Sonachala.

One attains this world, (*i.e.* the earth) at the first step, the middle world at the second step and the world of the *devas* at the third step. At the first step sins committed mentally are destroyed, at the second the sins committed by speech and at the third the sins committed by the body.

There are thousands of *ashrams* of *munis* and *siddhas* and abodes of *devas* around Me. I myself abide here always in the form of a *Siddha* worshipped by the *devas*. Let one imagine a divine abode gloriously existing within Me. What is known as Arunadri is really a Column of Effulgence. Meditating on this great *Linga* one should circumambulate it slowly. If one does so all sins will be expiated. One will not be born again and will certainly become eternally one with Sonachala.

The moment one takes a step with the intention of circumambulating Sonagiri the very earth becomes extremely pure by coming into contact with the dust of one's feet. At every point of the compass one should meditate and bring the palms together in praise and reverence. One should walk carefully, slowly and noiselessly. Before setting out a bath should be taken, clean clothes should be put on, sacred ash applied on the body, and *rudraksha* beads worn. While circumambulating one should meditate on Siva. Thousands of invisible *manus*, *devatas*, *siddhapurushas* and others accompany a devotee who circumambulates in this manner. Therefore a wise man should, even amidst a crowd, tread with great care regarding the Hill as divine. One may also walk in the company of devotees singing the sacred names of Siva and dancing. Alms should be given on the way according to one's means and one should remember Siva in the heart with love and devotion.

This Hill is incomprehensible, being beyond speech and thought. It is unapproachable, being a mass of fire. It is the Absolute and therefore called the Supreme.

The body of one who performs *anga-pradakshina* around this Hill becomes divine and immune to injury. The *devas* circumambulate Me everyday. The sun and other celestial bodies have obtained their lordship over the other planets by circumambulating Me.

A devotee who circumambulates the Hill on a Sunday penetrates the region of the Sun and attains Liberation. He gains the world of Siva. He who circumambulates the Hill on a Monday lives free from the afflictions of old age and death. He who circumambulates the Hill on a Tuesday is released from all debts and becomes an emperor. If *pradakshina* is done on Wednesday, he becomes omniscient and wise; on Thursday, he is worshipped by all the *devas* and attains fame as a *guru*. Circumambulation on a Friday brings prosperity and takes him to the abode of Vishnu; a Saturday *pradakshina* brings worldly success and averts the ill-effects threatened by the planets in one's horoscope. If those who suffer from physical and mental ailments, as well as those who are weak and emaciated, circumambulate Me, their ailments are cured.

The *nakshatras* (stars) and the *devatas* (deities) presiding over the planets favour those who circumambulate the Hill. *Tithi*, *karana, yoga, muhurta, hora* etc., (divisions of time) are also favourably disposed. The sound *pra* in the word *pradakshina* (circumambulation) means rooting out sins, *da,* granting desires, *kshi,* obliterating the fruits of *karma* and *na,* bestowing Liberation. This is the real meaning of the word *pradakshina*.

Even I circumambulate Arunadri, the divinely Effulgent *Linga* which is My form, in the company of *ganas*, *devas* and *rishis* at the time of the sacred *Uttarayana* (the winter solistice). I do so for the welfare of the world. Moreover Goddess Gowri will come here to do penance. She will become pure by circumambulating Me. Afterwards She will gain one half of My body. She will perform severe penance and circumambulate Me at the time of *pradosha* (the evening of the thirteenth day of both the waxing and the waning moon) on the day of *Kritika* (the day on which the moon is in conjunction with the star Pleiades) in the month of *Kartika* (the eight month of the Indian solar calendar which corresponds to November-December). The Goddess in the form of Apitakuchambika shall then merge in Me.

All the *devas* rejoice during the holy season of *Uttarayana*. During this season all the *devas*, *gandharvas*, *yakshas*, *siddhas* and *rakshasas* gather at this place, worship Me, make progress in their austerities and perform the rites which expiate all the sins committed by them in their previous lives. The day on which the holy season of *Uttarayana* commences is an auspicious day for men. Hence let them adore Me on that day and attain the goal of their lives.

One should never circumambulate the Hill on any kind of conveyance. For it is against *dharma*. Once upon a time a king named Dharmaketu who came from the world of Yama rode round the Hill on horseback. After completion of *pradakshina* his horse was transformed into a *Gananatha*. Amidst praises sung by the *devas* it left its master and gained the abode of Siva. Witnessing this the king repented and circumambulated the Hill on foot. Needless to say that he too joined the *ganas* and attained Siva's abode. Since then Indra and the thiry-three crore *devas* as well as Vishnu go round Arunachala on foot.

If the foot of one who circumambulates Arunachala bleeds, it will be wiped with the *mandara* flowers worn on Devendra's head. The foot which happens to be injured while circumambulating will be soothed by the *kumkum* (vermilion) from the body of Goddess Lakshmi.

On hearing all this Gowri said: O Sage! Kindly expound on the merits acquired by serving this Hill. Tell me the story of those fortunate persons who served this Hill with reverence and how they attained the goal of their lives. Thereupon Gautama said: I shall describe the merits acquired by serving this Hill as narrated by Parameswara Himself on a former occasion. A spider wove its web on one of the slopes of the Hill. This amounted to clothing the Hill. It gained the ability to recall its previous births. Poisonous insects move about harmlessly on the slopes. Those who light even a single lantern regularly for Arunachala become Self-Effulgent. A parrot built its nest on a tree close to Arunachala and kept in it some fireflies which dispelled the darkness all around it by their light. It therefore attained Liberation. A few cows were grazing on the slopes of the Hill. Their thoughts turned to their calves. Instantly milk dripped from their udders and drenched the slopes. As a result of this spontaneous *abhisheka* which they performed to Arunachala they attained Liberation. When a crow flew in search of prey its wings fanned the Hill. It attained Liberation immediately. *Devas* and *rishis* dwell close to Arunachala as trees with the object of avoiding future births.

If one constructs a *gopura* (a tower), a *sikbara* (spire), a road or a *mantapa* (pavilion), or digs a well in this place he will obtain what he desires. Let this *Linga* of fire which cannot be approached by mortals be worshipped on earth. Unnamulai Ambika, the Supreme Power, nourishes the entire world which is Her creation. The Mother of the universe is eternally young. Let those who desire to become eternally young worship Her.

Worship the Lord of Sonadri, the repository of immeasurable virtues, who grants boons and the source of all joys. Your desires will be fulfilled and you will join Sambhu. Your penance is meant for the welfare of the world. There is nothing which you desire for yourself. Let the austerities and *dharma* of the *rishis* flourish. *Devatas* do penance only to fulfill their desires. The goal of our lives will be reached by living near you when you are performing your penance. O Queen of all celestial beings! Everything will be accomplished by your penance.

On hearing these words of the *muni*, Goddess Gowri was extremely pleased. She praised him thus: What other penance is necessary? I have had your *darshan* and of Arunachala and have obtained your blessings. I have listened to its glory. This Earth is superior to *swarga*, for the Effulgent *Linga* abides here and it grants boons even to *devas*. Siva can be attained only by His Grace. His abode has been revealed to me. I shall adore Him at this very place and propitiate Him. I shall gain eternal union with Siva.

The Goddess then decided to perform penance devoutly in the presence of Gautama. At Gowri's behest a thatched hut was built for Her. The Goddess with Her slender form, lotus-like eyes, matted tresses, wearing a tree-bark and shining with the brilliance of a carbuncle was the very embodiment of penance. She followed the various scriptural injunctions and exhibited Her devotion to Her Lord in various ways, thus teaching the world the paths of *dharma* as laid down in the Vedas and *sastras*. Her slender body withstood the severity of penance without exhibiting the least trace of weariness.

# X. The Slaying of the Demon Mahishasura

BRAHMA continued: The *devas* who were oppressed by Mahishasura, a demon who had taken the form of a buffalo, came down to earth and sought refuge with the Goddess. They cried in fear, 'O Goddess! Save us!' When She asked what the matter was, Indra and the other *devas* folded their palms respectfully and told Her about their suffering at the hands of Mahishasura. They said:

Mahisha sports in the woods of Nandana with the *apsaras* (celestial nymphs), having brought under control Airavata (Indra's elephant) and other *dig-gajas* (elephants belonging to the eight cardinal points). He has taken possession of Uchaisravas (Indra's Horse) and other horses. He also keeps millions of goats which are the mounts of Agni, and allows his sons to ride them. He yokes the bison, the mount of Yama, to his chariot. *Siddhas* have been enslaved, are compelled to do his bidding and wait upon him. If there is anything in all the three worlds that he does not possess, he is not satisfied until he gets hold of it. As for us, we live in fear of him as his servitors and are compelled to obey his commands.

This *asura* (demon) is invincible. Having obtained a boon from Siva he is more powerful than *devas* and all others. Harrassed by Mahisha, the king of the seas wails in desperation and offers his jewels. With his horns Mahisha digs the mountains. His strength is unequalled. Nobody can oppose him. You will discover this yourself when you come to destroy him. You are the power (*shakti*) of Sambhu in the form of a woman. It is destined that he should be killed by you; for he has obtained a boon from Sambhu that no man shall kill him. Goddess! You must save us!

Hearing them cry out in fear in this manner, the Goddess in all graciousness assured them of Her protection. She spoke endearingly: *Devas*! My children! It is said that one of the objectives of doing penance is protection of those who seek refuge. Your enemy will perish in a short time. I shall kill that great *asura* by strategy. It is not right to kill one who is innocent. He who acts contrary to *dharma*, against those who abide by *dharma*, will die like an insect.

Their fears having vanished upon hearing these words of assurance, the *devas* bowed to the daughter of the mountain, and returned in peace to their abode. After their departure the lotus-eyed Gowri manifested herself as the power of resplendent delusion (*Mohini*), and appointed four noble *Bhairavis* to keep watch on all four sides of Arunagiri. These four celestial damsels, named Dundubhi, Satyavati, Anavami and Sundari, had followed Gowri to serve Her when She came away from the Kailasa Mountain. She now issued the following orders to them:

Admit only those who have come to worship Arunachala and are tired, hungry and thirsty. Others should not enter. She then appointed strong men to guard the boundaries of Arunachala and continued Her penance at Her *ashram*.

While She did penance in this manner, the place had plentiful rains. The crops grew lush and green. Even the creatures which are mutually hostile forgot their hostility. The *ashram* became a place for all creatures to live in harmony. Arunagiri was protected by guards for a distance of two *yojanas* all around. Everyone felt safe. Lust and violent passions were unknown. All the *munis* were pleased. They praised Gowri and Her *ashram* as if it were the world of Siva. She continued to practise Her austerities day and night, greatly rejoicing in attending to those matters which pleased Siva.

One day the arrogant Mahisha entered the forest of Arunachala which was far from his own country with the intention to hunt. He and his followers hunted the animals that roamed fearlessly in the forest. Seeing his warriors roaming about with bows, the animals fled in fear. Some of them took refuge in the *ashram* of the Goddess. The *asuras* were promptly prevented by the guards from entering the *ashram*. When they asked the reason, the guards replied: 'Gowri is doing penance here. Therefore She is bound to protect those who take shelter within these precincts. This is a place meant for *munis*. No one shall forcibly enter.' The *asuras* turned back, pondering on their next move. They then entered the *ashram* in the guise of birds and, sitting on the branches of the trees within the *ashram*, saw the Goddess. Afterwards they praised the enchanting beauty of the Goddess to Mahisha.

On hearing their words he was stricken with lust. Disguising himself as an old man he entered the *ashram* and was welcomed by the companions of the Goddess. He pretended to be pleased by their hospitality and asked them: 'Why are you doing penance here?' They said: '*Bala* (*lit.* maiden) has been doing penance here for a long time in order to obtain a husband. But She can never find one who possesses the qualities She desires. It seems that She has decided to marry only a valiant person who can perform great deeds.'

Upon hearing this Mahisha laughed and said to Gowri: 'O Maiden! Performer of penance! I seem to have come here only in answer to your prayer. Listen! I shall describe my glories. I am Mahisha the extremely valiant king of the *asuras*. All the three worlds are under my control. I alone possess such matchless valour. O maiden! I am the embodiment of love. I can give you every pleasure. Take me for your husband. I shall grant you the fruit of the austerities of all beings with the help of the wish-fulfilling tree. I can create even Visvakarma (the divine architect) by my power. I can create thousands of *kamadhenus* (wish-fulfilling cows) in a moment. Around me are the nine *nidhis* (repositories of precious objects) with the aid of which all desires can be instantly fulfilled.'

When the Goddess heard what he said, She remembered the prayer of the *devas*. Abandoning Her vow of silence She said jestingly: 'I will become the wife of only a valiant man. I have been doing penance for a long time with that object in view. If you are such a man, display your strength. If you fail, admit that you are weak.'

On hearing these words Mahisha became very angry. He roared: 'You are now as good as dead! Who are you to speak to me thus?' and sprang towards the Goddess with the object of killing Her. At his approach Gowri quickly transformed herself into Durga the fiery and invincible Goddess. As soon as Mahishasura saw the blazing *Maha Maya* before him, he made himself exceedingly huge like the Meru Mountain. He tore off mountain peaks and hurled them at Her and gathered around him his vast armies from all quarters. Hari and Sadasiva offered Goddess Durga five arrows each and Brahma four. The *dikpalakas,* the *devas*, the mountains and the seas all offered their respective ornaments, weapons and missiles to the Goddess and praised Her splendour. She put on armour and immediately mounted a lion.

Being unable to look at the all-pervasive Effulgence and afraid to face the mighty Goddess, Mahisha ran.

Thereupon Gowri thought that the wicked Mahishasura should be killed only by a stratagem: 'Just as hunters prod animals to make them enraged and turn about, even so I shall make him angry by sending some clever messengers and make him return at once to the battlefield. Those who are extremely unrighteous will not listen to the words of *dharma*. For, if they do so, their way of living will be adversely affected. On the contrary, if he listens to the words of *dharma* and becomes peaceful he shall be saved. Then he will not violate *dharma*. Those who do penance do not become angry. Penance should make one free from anger. One should not do anything which is not in accordance with *dharma*.

Reflecting thus, Goddess Gowri sent a monkey-faced *muni* named Suraguru to Mahisha. She said to him: 'Maharshi Vanaramukha! Endowed with the power of *maya* which I shall bestow upon you, you shall go to Mahisha and make him return quickly with the following words:

' "Do not oppress anyone around Arunadri as you wickedly intend to do. The valour of wicked persons who do so will be completely destroyed in a moment. The afflictions of the age of *kali* and troubles from *asuras* have no place there. For it is a holy and auspicious place meant for the devotees of Siva. By the merit you have acquired in some former life you now possess valour and good fortune. Let not your demonaic nature make you fall into the fire of Arunachala like a moth. The boon acquired by you by the grace of Siva and through your penance will be completely burnt and destroyed like twigs in a forest fire. Only those who follow *dharma* and are devotees of Siva may live there. Those who oppress others will develop all kinds of diseases. You have more power than others and your valour cannot be challenged by anyone. Hence you should not lose it by your rashness.

' "I too saw the maiden coveted by you. She is truly *abala* (destitute). Still, as She is under the protection of the Lord of Arunachala, She cannot be conquered. If, however, you do not listen to my advice and come to battle, She will destroy all the boons which have made you an arrogant oppressor.

' "Station all your armed forces in front of the Goddess. She will destroy them in a moment. When you are killed by Her weapons you and your followers may or may not attain Liberation. Who can divine the plan of the Lord? One is bound to reap the fruit of the deeds prompted by one's inherent tendencies. No one can prevent it." In this manner teach him his own *dharma* and make him abandon what is not *dharma*.'

When Vanaramukha who was sent by the Goddess with these instructions delivered the message to Mahisha, the latter was enraged and approached the *muni* with the intention of killing him, but the *muni* escaped through the power of *maya*. The wicked demon then gathered all his armed forces and prepared for battle. His forces came from all quarters and surrounded Arunagiri.

As soon as Gowri saw the *asura* army, She brought into existence fierce warriors, *bhuta ganas*, and monstrous creatures. Then the Goddess blew Her conch. As soon as the *asuras* heard the sound and saw Her, they shot a host of arrows from all sides in order to show their valour. But the Goddess stopped them all with Her arrows. The *bhutas* and *vetalas* created by the Goddess fought fiercely. The attendant goddesses killed many of the enemies quickly. Amidst the dead bodies of the *asuras*, the *bhutas* danced in victory. The Goddess stood fully armed alongwith Her maidens, Dundubhi, Satyavati, Anavami and Sundari.

As soon as Mahisha saw Her he became enraged. He pierced the clouds with the tip of his horns, darted his flame-like tongue hither and thither, butted the earth with his horns, pawed the earth with his hooves raining clouds of dust on all sides and roared fiercely. He lifted his hairy tail and shattered many of the weapons of the *devas* who became frightened. Then he turned towards the beautiful Bhavani who was mounted on a lion and charged towards Her only to meet his doom!

Mahisha rained arrows and many other weapons on Goddess Gowri. But She stopped them all at a distance with Her arrows and pierced his body in many places. While assailed thus with discs, axes, maces, spears and many other weapons he disappeared suddenly and came back a moment later in the form of a fierce lion. Roaring terribly he raged about the battlefield attacking with his teeth and sharp claws. Everytime he was defeated, he took a new form. Thus he came as a tiger, then an elephant and then a fierce warrior with a sword. The Goddess who was carrying a sword, shield and a disc fought with him and cut off his head. But he resumed his form of Mahisha and fought with Her tirelessly.

Then the *devas* and *munis* approached Gautama who praised the Mother of the world and reminded Her of Her innate glory. Gautama pleaded with Bhagavati to eliminate the *asura* immediately.

The Goddess pierced Mahisha with Her trident. His body was as big as a mountain range but he could not withstand the valour of the Goddess. He fell and rolled on the ground but could not extricate himself from the trident. He looked like a red sea with blood flowing from his face and limbs. The Goddess cut off his head with a sharp sword and stood dancing upon him. Seeing this the *siddhas*, *gandharvas* and *Maharshis* hailed Her as Goddess Durga. Indra, the king of the *devas*, bowed down before Her and with folded hands he praised the Goddess. He prayed that Her form as Mahishasura Mardhani (the destroyer of Mahisha) should be a source of prosperity and happiness for all creation.

When the Goddess was praised in this manner and worshipped by Indra and adored by the *rishis*, She complied with their request and said, "Let it be so". She created an image bearing all kinds of weapons and installed it in the world of the *devas*. Then She took Her place here again assuming Her tranquil form surrounded by Her companions. She looked at the severed head and neck of Mahisha. Seeing a *linga* there She quietly took it with the object of worshipping it. She looked at the blood smeared *linga* carefully for a long time. When She did so the *linga* stuck to Her hand. She could not remove it! She exclaimed: "Why has this happened?" In distress She went to

Maharshi Gautama and said: "This devotee of Siva was killed by me. I am therefore overcome by sorrow."

Pained at what She had done She continued:

"O Sage! You know all the *dharmas*! I wanted to protect the *devas*. So I assured them of my protection. While fulfilling my promise, though meant for protecting *dharma*, I have committed an act of *adharma*. This *linga* which was around his neck clings to my hand. How shall I expiate the sin of killing a devotee of Siva? Until I obtain the Grace of Siva I shall go on a pilgrimage with this *linga* and do penance. Afterwards I shall bathe in the holy waters flowing at places sacred to Siva and expiate my sin." Gautama who was well-versed in the *dharma* of Siva said: "Gowri! Do not fear that you killed a devotee of Siva by mistake. Mahisha could not be conquered by the *devas* not because he had the good fortune to possess the *linga*, but because he had to be killed only by you, the beloved of Siva. He roused the anger of *Maharshis* who were the devotees of Siva, hated them and scorned them. Consequently he was cursed by them thus: 'As you behave like a buffalo you shall become a wild bison.' And he immediately became Mahisha (bison). But when he bowed to them, praised them and begged for release from his curse, they were pleased to give him the following advice: 'Although you have become a bison, by Siva's command, you will be slain by the Goddess herself. You need not be depressed at your plight. Who is not punished for scorning the *siddhas* who are actually Siva? Although you have, on account of your sin become a bison, you will be released from the curse through the grace of the *siddhas*.'

"O Gowri, Mahisha has been killed by you because of your penance. If necessary you may for the sake of pleasing Siva, have *darshan* of Arunachala, the Effulgent *Linga*. Mahisha was a devotee of the Lord of Arunadri in his previous birth. Afterwards he became a wild buffalo but somehow he acquired a *linga*. Who is there in the three worlds who can kill the wearer of a *linga*?

"It is said that a *linga* which is worn without proper initiation will bring ruin upon the wearer. Or perhaps, he swerved away from the virtuous path by evil counsels. There is no doubt that he has been liberated by coming into contact with your lotus feet, as a result of the austerities performed by him in his former lives, by the remembrance of his real nature and the wearing of the *linga*. In any case, the sight of this noble Hill is the sure means of expiating all sins.

"Goddess! This sin can be expiated in the following manner: You must bring some followers of *Saiva Siddhanta* and settle them here. You must then make all the holy waters meet here and form a single holy pond, in which you must bathe wearing the *linga* and uttering the *aghamarshana mantra* (*mantra* which expiates sins). You must bathe thrice daily and, at the end of one month, perform *Deva Yaga* (sacrifice for the gods) and worship the Lord of Arunadri."

When Bhagavati learnt from the *muni* this secret about Siva, She took the necessary steps for bathing in such a holy pond and expiating Her sins.

# XI. The Goddess Joins Siva

WHEN Gautama spoke in this manner Gowri's doubts were cleared. A sweet voice was then heard coming from the sky. It said: Daughter of the mountain! You need not go anywhere else to expiate your sin. Split open a rock with your sword. All the nine *tirthas* namely, the Ganga, the Yamuna, the Sindhu, the Godavari, the Saraswati, the Narmada, the Kaveri, the Sonanadi and the Sonanadam will appear in that cleft. Bathe in them uttering the sin-destroying *mantra* in the month of *Asvija* (October-November) in the asterism of *Jyeshta* (Antares). You must bathe in this holy water and at the end of the month install on the bank of that holy *tirtha* the *linga* in your hand consecrating it for the welfare of the world.

If anyone bathes in that *tirtha* and worships that *linga* he will undoubtedly be free from the three kinds of misery.

Celebrate a festival for ten days with the maidens named Anumati, Bala, Sinivali, Guha and Yatri, take the final bath when the star *Krittika* (Pleiades) is in ascension and worship Sonachala in the evening in the prescribed manner. I shall then reveal to you my own Effulgent form. You must do this solely for the welfare of the world.

Goddess Gowri thereupon proceeded to do what the Maharshi and the voice from the sky had asked Her to do. She caused by Her powers, lotuses resembling Her eyes and *utpala* flowers resembling Her smile to bloom in that *tirtha*. The world was blessed by Her presence there. Everyone's desires were fulfilled and there was contentment everywhere. But Her mind was agitated on account of Her separation from Sambhu.

At the end of one month the Goddess celebrated a festival. On the evening when *Krittika* was in conjunction with the Moon in the month of *Karthika* (November-December), She propitiated the Lord of Arunadri with all the prescribed offerings and offering of water (*arghya*). The Mother of the world then prayed, "Visvarupa! God in the form of Sonachala! Effulgent one! *Linga* in the form of a hill! Remover of all sins! Obeisance to Thee. Thy glory could not be realised even by Brahma and Vishnu as Thou art truly fiery. But Thou hast cooled down for the welfare of the world."

When the Goddess stood praying thus, Arunadri manifested himself as an Effulgent Column blazing in all directions. He appeared as a supreme Effulgence resembling the rising of crores of suns, or a crore of full-moons or world-consuming fires. The *munis* (sages) and the Goddess prostrated before it with extreme veneration. While the Goddess stood overcome with joy, the Lord of Arunadri rose out of that Effulgence in a golden form with a bluish throat and said: I am pleased with you, for you have performed penance and austerities at the places specified by me. You have now directly realised my radiant form. Being the mother of the world you protect the world for various reasons. What is your wish? Beloved one! Your doubts and fears have vanished the moment you saw my splendour!

You have not incurred any sin by the act of killing Mahisha. Moreover, as you have looked at Sonachala, you have expiated all your sins. Your eyes have become blessed. You engaged a foster-mother to suckle your son. And, instead of being with him, you were here as Unnamulai (mother of the unsuckled breasts) in the month of *Karthika* for the protection of your devotees. You shall therefore be worshipped as *Apitakuchambika* (The Sanskrit equivalent for Unnamulai). After completing this worship for the welfare of the devotees you shall meditate upon me.

When Siva spoke these words, Ambika bowed to him and prayed: Deva of *devas*! Every year on this *Krittika* day of the full moon, pray, reveal that divine form which was devoutly worshipped by me and the *devas* on this auspicious day so that all may be protected from adversity. Mahadeva said, "So be it"."

The Goddess then went round the hill along with Her companions. As She did so Arunachala shone like an emerald and Her sacred body was enveloped by the lustre of the Hill. As She walked slowly, the lustre of Her lotus feet made the earth look as if it had been strewn with lotus petals. Her radiant looks were like blossoms of *nilotpala* (blue lotus) scattered by worshippers all round Sonadri.

Goddess Gowri was devoutly walking round the Hill as if She were walking round the ceremonial marriage *havan* with the object of attaining union with Siva. She was joined at each step by Brahma, Vishnu and their consorts Saraswati and Lakshmi respectively, the *devas*, the *dikpalakas* and their consorts and the celestial maidens with their fragrant offerings. It appeared, as if by Her austerities She was appeasing the hill of fire. Constantly remembering Mahadeva She gave spiritual instruction to the divine *rishis*.

# XII. The Lord Grants the Boon of Supreme Excellence to Arunachala

BRAHMA said: The Mother of the world bowed to the Destroyer of the three cities and prayed that She should attain union with Him. Noted for Her sweet words, She prayed very devoutly in this manner for the welfare of the world, "Let not this form of Thine which charms the eye and the mind be ever abandoned by Thee. As this form of Thine is enchanting, auspicious for the world and is full of divine bliss, let everyone always have Thy *darshan*. Instead of Thy former appearance of matted hair, wearing the serpent round the neck, holding the skull of Brahma, smearing ash from the *Rudra Bhoomi* (cremation ground), pray, assume the form of the *Maha Purusha,* the Eternal Bridegroom, adorning divine garlands, perfumes, robes and gem-set ornaments. Great Lord! Let *deva* and *gandharva* maidens adore Thee, dancing and singing to the accompaniment of musical instruments. Let Thy devotees also adore Thee unceasingly. Let this vision of our united form *Ardhanareeswara,* be always, by Thy Grace, capable of inspiring intense devotion, of bestowing prosperity and of fulfilling all desires."

The Lord of Arunachala listened to these words of the Goddess and fulfilled Her wishes. With great affection He said, "An Asura named Pulaka once performed austerities, assuming the form of an animal for that purpose, and obtained a boon from me. Thereupon his body began to emit a fragrant smell. Due to this the celestial damsels were attracted to him. This enraged the *devas* who then appealed to me. Thereupon I summoned the *asura* and ordered him to abandon his body. He bowed to me, adored me with devotion and said, 'Lord of the *devas*! I shall abandon this body according to Thy command. This fragrant substance is fit to be adorned by Thee alone. Thou must therefore graciously accept it as my offerring. O Lord of the world! I shall now happily abandon this body of mine. Let this perfume be worn by Thee and by the Goddess. Let my descendants, *i.e.,* civet cats, acquire this fragrance by virtue of my sacrifice'. I granted him the boon. Pulaka then entrusted his life to me and abandoned his body. I am now offerring you this perfume. You may wear it."

Parvati then narrated the greatness of the Ekamra *linga* which was installed by Her during Her penance at Kancheepuram.

Brahma continued: On hearing this the Lord of Sonachala granted all the boons the Goddess asked for. The Lord himself now appears as Sonachala (the red Hill) which is adored by the world. It grants every boon. Shambu Himself, with Gowri shines as Arunachala. Those who have *darshan* of it or meditate upon it, attain liberation. All kinds of wealth accrue to those who hear of the glory of Arunachala. Those who remember Arunachala will become pure in mind. They shall be absolved of their *karmas*. A mere *darshan* of Arunachala will grant the benefit of bathing in all the holy *tirthas* and performing all *yajnas* and *yagas*. He will obtain the grace of Sadasiva. Among the various places on earth which are sacred to Siva, it is only at this place that Sambhu fell in love with His own majestic and magnificent form. He lost the desire to dwell at Kailasa. He asked Parvati, all the *rishis* and *devas* to come and perform penance, austerities and all rituals that are laid down in the scriptures. In Bharatavarsha *dharma* is cherished because of the presence of Arunachala. Devotees whose sins have all been destroyed in the blaze of Arunachala live in bliss. Arunachala fulfills the wishes of those who adore Him with circumambulation, prostration and perform austerities. A single *darshan* of Arunachala pleases Him much more than austerities, offerings and *yagnas* performed at other *kshetras*. The Vedas and the epics in the form of hills surrounding Arunachala pay their obeisance to Him. Neither I nor Vishnu with all our skill can adequately describe the glory of Arunachala. Myself, Vishnu, and the *devas* always worship it while remaining invisible. Disease, distress, mental worry and other miseries incidental to the dark age of *kaliyuga* do not affect those who always adore Arunachala. The power of Arunachala nullifies the influence of planets. I have thus described to the best of my ability the glory of Arunachala which bestows Liberation in a trice on one who contemplates upon Him.

Suta said: When Sage Sanaka heard with rapt attention the glorious and nectar-sweet story of Arunagiri that flowed from the lips of Brahma, he was full of bliss.

## End of Part I

# PART - II

This part is taken from a portion of *Skanda Purana* where Nandi, the mount of Lord Siva, narrates the glory of Arunachala to the immortal *rishi* Markandeya. This version is slightly different from that given in Part One. Readers may find certain details repetitive, nevertheless, it must be borne in mind that it serves to emphasise the greatness of Arunachala. This is exactly the aim of this work.

# I. GLORY OF PLACES AND *TIRTHAS* SACRED TO SIVA

VYASA said: The ascetics (*munis*) who lived in the Naimisa forest asked Bhagavan Suta: Of all places sacred to Siva which is the greatest? Kindly enlighten us.

Suta said: O ascetics! I shall tell you what Sage Markandeya formerly learnt from Nandikesvara. Listen. Markandeya said to Nandikesvara: Nandikesvara! I listened with devotion and faith to the story of Madhyamesvara narrated by you. I request you to continue. There is nothing unknown to you in the three worlds.

Nandikesvara said: O best of ascetics! There is one place which corresponds to your description and which is the best of all sacred places and exists for the welfare of all beings, movable and immovable. It is ordained by *Isvara* that all *jivas* should be born according to their *karmas*. What you desire to know should prove beneficial to these *jivas*. Otherwise they will not obtain liberation from *samsara* even after the lapse of a crore of aeons (*kalpas*). Unfructified *karma* binds them to the vicious cycle of birth and death. There is no escape from it. Is there any means other than absolute knowledge to escape from this cycle? I have already described the places which are sacred to Siva, the benefits derived by residing at those places and the names of the *rishis* who live there. Some live on the banks of the Ganga, the Saraswati, the Yamuna, the Sona, the Narmada, the Godavari, the Gomati the Haimavati (name of the Ganga before it reaches the plains), the Krishna, the Tungabhadra, the Upaveni, the Pennai, the Kaveri, the Vaigai, the Tamraparni, the Mandakini, the Sipra (the river at Avanti), the Sarayu, the Murala, the Airavati, the Yadukangkshi, the Kanyakumari, the Tamasa, the Varuna, the Vipasa, the Sadadruti, the Charmani, the Bhimarati, the Bindusaras, the Pampa, the Bhairavi, the Kausiki, the Maliri, the Gandhavati, the Manasa, the Achhoda, the Indradyumna, the Manikarnika, the Varada, the Patala Ganga, the Saravati, the Lohati, the Kalama, the Vitasta, the Chandrabhaga, the Surala, the Payoshni, the Madhumati and the Pinakini Kasi, Panchakrosa, Avimukti. Others live on the seashore, or on islands, or in the sacrificial halls erected on the banks of the Sindhu, or at the places where rivers enter the sea.

Varanasi where *Isvara* is worshipped along with Goddess Visalakshi, and Kapalamochana, the place sacred to Kalabhairava are particularly sacred. Those who die at Sri Kasi become *Rudras*. Gaya and Prayaga are stated to be places where one attains everything spiritual. Offering rice to the manes of one's ancestors (*pitris*) at these places releases them from suffering. Badarikasrama, where Tryambaka accompanied by the Goddess was worshipped by Nara and Narayana, confers merit on worshippers. Maheswara carrying the bow named *saranga* and accompanied by the Goddess is worshipped by the *rishis* at Naimisaaranya. Amarnath is also very sacred. Isa abides at Omkar in the company of Goddess Chandi. I have already told you about the famous place known as Pushkara. Rajogandhi Deva abides there in the company of Goddess Puruhoota.

Similarly Astadesa and Raticha are installed at Ashadi. Mundi Deva and Goddess Dandika Devi at Dandimundi; Lakulisa and the most auspicious Goddess named Ananga at Lakula; Paresa and Goddess Bhooti at Parabhuti; Sukshmesa and Sukkhmesvari at Aralesvara; Sankara and Mangala at Gaya; Sthanu and Sthanupriya at Kurukshetra; Ugra and Goddess Ugra Devi at Kanakhal; Swayambhu Siva and Goddess Swayambhuvi at Talaka. I have already described Attahasa where Surya worshipped Siva and attained the Supreme goal of his life; Krithivasa which is superior to Kailasa; Srisaila where Sri Mallikarjuna and Bhramaramba are worshipped by Brahma; Kalahasti the abode of Sankara and Jnanaprasoonambika, worshipped by Vyasa and Kancheepura, sacred to Ekamresvara and Kamakshi. Nataraja is worshipped by Patanjali at Chidambaram; the broken tusk of Airavata (Indra's elephant) grew again when it worshipped Siva at

Tiruvenkadu. Sri Rama installed *Ramalinga* at Rameswaram. Siva is being worshipped at Jambukesvaram for the welfare of the whole world. *Isvara* is always present at Vriddhachala on the bank of the Manimukta. At Madhyarjuna, Siva who is accompanied by Gowri, grants all boons. Those who die at Somanatha are not born again. At Siddhavata the Effulgent *Jyotir Linga* is worshipped by *siddhas*. Hari worshipped Valinikesvara at Kamalalaya and obtained Lakshmi for his consort. Brahma and Vishnu worship Siva at Tirukkazhukundram for attaining Liberation. The Lord of Parvati abides at Thonipuri in a boat during the great deluge which comes at the end of *kaliyuga*. In olden days Indrajit installed Siva in the temple at Brahmapuram on the bank of Aryapushkarani. At Srikota, the temple of wisdom, people worship Chandramaulisvara to expiate their sins. Parasurama worshipped Siva at Gokarna. If one worships Siva at Tripurantaka one need not fear *naraka* (hell). Devotees who worship Him at Kalanjana become sinless and are released from *samsara*. At Prabhasa, He bestows upon devotees everlasting benefits. Daksha worshipped *Isvara* at Vedaranya with the object of expiating the sin committed by him and attained Liberation. Those who worship Isa at Hemakuta need not fear rebirth. At Venuvana, Ambika manifested herself as a pearl inside a bamboo. It is a place where one's sins are expiated. At Jvalamukhi the Goddess worshipped Kalarudra. Ganapati worshipped Siva at Patravata. At Nyagrodharanya, Kala and Siva vied with each other in dancing. Anjaneya worshipped Mrityunjaya at Gandhamadana. Panini became a great grammarian by worshipping Sambhu at Goparvata and obtained His grace. At Veerakoshta, Valmiki became a great poet by the grace of Siva. At Mahatirtha, Siva taught the Vedas to Brahma, Vishnu and others. Indra obtained his *Vajrayudha* (thunderbolt) at Mayavaram. At Madurai on the banks of the Vaigai, Siva manifested as Sundaresvara. At Kumbakonam, Goddess Ganga manifests herself in the month of *Masi* by Siva's grace and removes all sins. Skanda obtained at Tryambaka the spear called *sakti* with which he killed Taraka. Trisanku, who was born in a low caste, worshipped Siva at Sripatala to purify himself. Sambhu punished Yama (the god of death) at Kadambapuri to save you. Siva bestowed his grace upon Patikantha at Avinashi. At Rakta Kanna, He granted to Mitra and Varuna the boon by which they were saved from rebirth. Vairochana Mahabali worships Siva at Hatakeswara while living in *patala* (the nether world). Kailasa is another place sacred to Siva; Kubera worships Him there.

# II. The Sacred Arunachala

HAVING narrated the glory of various places sacred to Siva, Nandikesvara asked Markandeya, "You have now listened to all that I have said. What more do you wish to hear?" On hearing this, Markandeya the ascetic placed his head upon Nandikesvara's feet with devotion and prayed as follows:

"Bhagavan! Please do not evade my question. Your grace is the proof of my single-minded devotion to you. Each of the places mentioned by you so far has, no doubt, its particular efficacy, but which is the place that has the combined efficacy of all the sacred places? Please say which is that place, by remembering which knowingly or unknowingly even once, all beings moving as well as stationary attain Liberation.

"It is described in all the Vedas and *puranas* and elsewhere, that this earth is the place most suitable for those who wish to reach *swarga* and attain liberation. All *karmas* are efficacious only for those who live on this earth. You have explained that their results are of three kinds *viz.,* (1) worldly pleasures, (2) pleasures of *swarga* and (3) Liberation (*kaivalya*). The first two will come to an end as soon as the merit acquired by a person is exhausted, but the third does not depend upon performance of *karmas*. Therefore it will not come to an end. It has been stated by you that true knowledge is the only means of attaining it.

"However, absolute knowledge cannot be acquired by all embodied beings. Which is that place where true knowledge can be acquired without book learning, merely by worship of Siva? Please tell me which is that place where pure knowledge is attained by practising but a few religious rituals, the place where even lay men without any kind of scholarship can evolve spiritually by merely smearing sacred ash, wearing *rudraksha* beads and contemplating on Siva? Which is that place where all residents overcome obstacles and attain knowledge without any conscious effort? At which place do even the wicked, the lowliest of animals and inanimate objects attain Godhead?

"This is not only my prayer but also that of all the *Rishis* present here viz., Pulaha, Pulastya, Vasishta, Marichi, Agastya, Dadhichi, Nagru, Bhrigu, Atri, Jabali, Jaimini, Daumya, Jamadagni, Upayaja, Yaja, Bharata, Arvarivata, Pippaladha, Kanya, Kumuda, Upamanyu, Kumudaksha, Kutsa, Vatsa, Varatantu, Vibhandaka, Vyasa, Kanvarishi,

Kandul Mandavya, Matanga, Kukshi, Mandakarni, Chandal Kausika, Sandilya, Sakatayana, Satatapa, Manucchanda, Garga, Saubhari, Romasa, Apastamba, Prithustamba, Bhargava, Udanga, Parvata, Bharadvaja, Dasya, Danta, Svetaketu, Kaundinya, Pundarika, Raibhya, Trinabindu, Valmiki, Narada, Vahni, Dridhamanyu, Bodhayana, Kapota, Harita, Mrikandu, the extremely irritable Durvasa, Jalapada, Sakti, Gangavariya, Natanda, Devadatta, Nyangu, Susruta, Agnivesya, Galava, Matutva, Lokakshi, Visravas, Saindhava, Sumantu, Sisupayana, Maudgalya, Padya, Chyavanal Matura, Rishyasringa, Ekapada, Krauncha, Dridha, Gomukha, Devala, Angiras, Vamadeva, Aurva, Patanjali, Kapinjala, Sanatkumara, Sanaka, Sanandana, Sanatana, Hiranyanabha, Vatasana known as Satya, Suhota, Maitreya, Pushpajit, Satyatapa, Salishva, Saisira, Nidagha, Udatya, Samvarta, Saulkayani, Parasara, Vaisampayana, Kausalya, Saradvata, Kapidhvaja, Kusasvarchika, Kaivalya, Yajnavalkya, Asvalayana, Krishnatapottama, Anantakaruna, Amalakapriya, Charaka, Pavitra, Kapila, Kanachi, Nara-Narayana and many other *Maharshis*.

"You have crossed the ocean of all the *agamas*. Moreover you pervade all the worlds. Therefore kindly enlighten us. Whom else can we approach? All *agamas* and *puranas* can be learnt only from Paramesvara or Parvati or Skanda, or from you. Your kindness shows that you are aware of our devotion. Please kindly reveal to us the secret."

Having said thus, Markandeya and the other ascetics prostrated before Nandikesvara and awaited his answers eagerly. Nandikesvara looked at Markandeya, the best of devotees who had pleased Siva by his devotion.

Hearing the words of Markandeya, Nandikesvara nodded his head and said, "Yes, there is such a place on earth!" The thought of Arunachala crossed his mind and he went into *samadhi*. With tear filled eyes and his whole frame shaking with emotion, he said:

"O best of ascetics! I was only testing you. If I do not divulge the secret to you to whom shall I divulge it? Is there anyone like you in the world who follows the *dharma* of Siva? Is there anyone other than you who can gain everlasting life by the grace of Siva? It is only for your sake that Siva became angry and punished Yama who came to claim your life. The entire *dharma* of Siva is already known to you. I shall tell you about that sacred place. Only devotees of Siva are entitled to hear about that place. Now listen attentively.

"In the *Dravida* country (South India), there is this place, most sacred to Siva known as Arunachala. It extends to three *yojanas* all round. It is the heart of the earth. It is the favourite of Siva. There he has assumed the form of a Hill. He took the form of Arunachala for the welfare of the world. It is the abode of all the *siddhas, maharshis, devas, vidyadharas, yakshas, gandharvas,* and *apsaras*. It is regarded superior to the Meru, the Kailasa and the Mandara mountains by all. Since all creatures living there attain Liberation effortlessly, even the residents of *svarga* prefer to dwell there. The trees growing there have the good fortune of worshipping Hara in the form of this noble Hill with their leaves, flowers and fruits and are therefore superior to the wish-fulfilling and other trees which grow in *svarga*. Even hunters who are violent gain the imperishable merit derived from circumambulating the Hill when they go round this Hill while hunting. The rainwater falling from the clouds on its top is superior to the Ganga which flows from the Himalayas. Even the birds which sing there, and the reeds and bamboos which rub noisily against one another enjoy a status which *yakshas*, *gandharvas* and *kinnaras* cannot attain. The fireflies which give some light to those who walk there in darkness reach the abode of Siva. As the trees growing on the slopes of this hill have the good fortune of union with the Lord unhindered, they scorn even the Goddess, one of whose names is Aparna (leafless). The stars which pass over the top of this Hill attain thereby the goal of their existence. They do not seek even Chandra (the Moon). The wild animals roaming about the slopes of this Hill do not care even for the deer within their reach. Suffice it to say that even children and the young ones of the animals are envied by Ganesa and Guha if they happen to touch the foot of this Hill. The lions, tigers and elephants which live and die there are welcomed by the Lord of Sonadri and held in great esteem by Him.

"This immovable Hill is thus Sambhu Himself. The trees, the groves and the herbs growing on it are His matted locks. Its bright, conspicuous peak and the two peaks on either side, which are like the Sun and the Moon, are symbolic of His three eyes. The blue streams of water flowing from the top of this Hill during the rainy season are symbolic of His blue throat. 'The One with a thousand feet and a thousand eyes', is how the Lord is described in the Vedas. These are not mere words. Their truth can be directly perceived here in the form of this Hill. For, innumerable are the streams that flow from the top of this Hill which represents the head of the Bearer of the Ganga. The white clouds which settle in a circle round the middle of the Hill symbolise Siva as mounted on the bull. The dark clouds that settle on the peak show Him to be blue-throated. As this Hill is immovable, Siva came to be known as the Immovable one, Sthanu. Because of its imposing appearance He is described as the Great One, Bhima. As it is not possible to pass over this Hill, Siva is known as the formidable one, Ugra. The tiny rivulets on its sides are Takshaka and Ananta belonging to the hoard of serpents worn by Him as ornaments. The eight corners of this Hill represent His eight aspects *(Ashtamurti)*.

"In the distant past Parvati performed austerities here, pleased Siva and won His left half. Isa was enshrined in the form of a *linga* by Gowri on the *Pavalakkunru* (the Coral hillock), an eastern spur of Arunachala. That *linga* is capable of bestowing worldly benefits as well as Liberation. Durga, the slayer of Mahisha, abides there by the orders of Goddess Gowri. She removes all obstacles and graciously enables devotees to have vision of their personal deities and the person doing *mantra japa* attains the fruit of his *japa* (*mantrasiddhi*). In Gowri's *ashram* there is a *tirtha* known as *Khadga tirtha* (the *tirtha* made by the sword of Gowri). The five great sins of those who bathe in it are destroyed. The *linga* known as Papanasana (destroyer of sins) which was worshipped by goddess Durga, destroys all sins.

"By committing forbidden acts in Arunachala, a Pandya king, Vajrangada lost his power. Afterwards he attained union with Siva through devotion to the Hill. Two *vidyadharas* named Kantisali and Kaladhara were cursed by Durvasa. They got rid of the curse by circumambulating this Hill. There is no sacred place comparable to Sonadri, no *mantra* comparable to *Panchakshara*, no *dharma* comparable to the *dharma* of Mahesvara, no knowledge (*jnana*) comparable to the knowledge of Siva *(Sivajnana)*, no protective amulet comparable to the *Vedic* incantation, the *Rudram*, no devotee of Siva comparable to Vishnu, no righteous conduct comparable to devotion, no saviour comparable to the *Guru*, no ornament comparable to the *rudraksha*, no scripture (*sastra*) comparable to the *agamas* of Siva, no leaf comparable to the *bilva* leaf, no flower comparable to jasmine, no happiness comparable to dispassion, no supreme state comparable to Liberation. Neither Kailasa nor Meru nor Mandhara is comparable to Arunachala. For the former are only the abodes of Siva whereas this Hill is Siva Himself."

On hearing these words of Nandikesvara, Markandeya bowed to him and prayed: "What are the *karmas* which lead human beings to *samsara* and what *karmas* lead to hell? What are the acts by which sins can be expiated? Kindly explain."

# III. Sins and Their Consequences

NANDIKESVARA continued:

One who possesses the quality of *sattva* (purity and goodness, symbolised by white colour) is rare in this world. Generally people possess the qualities of *rajas* (passion and activity, symbolised by red) and *tamas* (inertia and dullness, symbolised by black). One who possesses the *sattvic* quality alone attains Liberation in due course while others are ordained by Brahma the Creator to take birth repeatedly and consigned to hell for their evil deeds. There are various kinds of hells. They are as follows:

One who kills a *brahmin* suffers torments in *maharourava* and other hells and takes birth afterwards as an ass, a dog, a pig or a *chandala* (outcaste). The *brahmin* who takes intoxicating drinks suffers torments for a time in the hell known as *raurava* and is then born as an insect or worm or a bird. He who steals the property of a *brahmin* becomes a *brahmarakshasa* (demon) and in his next life suffers for want of the things that he stole. One who covets another man's wife is tortured in the forest of *asipatra* (leaves made of swords) for a long time, and is reborn as a eunuch. He who covets his *Guru's* wife is first tortured by Yama's minions who tie him to a red hot iron pillar and suffers for a long time in the hell known as *kalasutra*. The poisoner has to suffer in a terrible (*ghora*) hell; the slanderer in the extremely terrible hell (*mahaghora*); the hater of *dharma* in the hell known as *avisa*; the deceiver in *karala*; the secret sinner in the hell called *sambara*; the liar in a frightful hell; the stealer of money in *asishora*; the malicious man in *vajranaraka*; the *brahmin* who eats meat in the hell called *tarala*; the stealer of temple property in *dahana*; the plunderer of others' property in *ghoraghora*; the traitor to parents in *tokshna*; the murderer of a child in the hell *chanda*; the murderer of a woman in *kulam*; the despiser of *mantra japa* in *tapana*; the slaughterer of a horse is suffocated to death; the slaughterer of the cow suffers in the hell called *dhruna*. In these hells sinners are bound with ropes by the minions of Yama, struck with cudgels and pierced with spears. They are pecked at by vultures and birds, bitten by serpents and attacked by dogs, tigers and lions. Their limbs are torn asunder, or cut to pieces and their eyes are gouged with sharp weapons. They are whipped, pierced with needles, fried in oil and made to carry heavy loads. The murderer of a *brahmin* is reborn as a consumptive, the drunkard as a person with decayed teeth, the stealer of gold with decayed nails, the paramour of the *Guru's* wife with skin diseases. The slanderer of the Vedas is born as a *chandala.* One who bears false witness suffers in his next life from diseases of the eye, one who acquires learning by deceit is dumb in his next life, the stealer of books becomes blind, the lover of others' wives becomes lame, the slanderer of others becomes deaf. The violator of customary practices is reborn as a pig, the thief with diseased tongue. The inhospitable man suffers in his next birth from pain in his cheeks, he who dallies with women at forbidden times suffers from diabetes and the eater of forbidden food from a foul-smelling mouth.

He who shows disrespect to others is reborn as a slave, the destroyer of ponds and gardens as an ass, the person who does not abide by his promise has a short span of life, the speaker of harsh words is born as a dog, the hater of Vishnu as a chameleon and the hater of Siva as a rat. One should realise the consequences of sinful acts and then perform rites for expiation in the temple of Arunachala.

After learning from Nandikesvara about the numerous kinds of tortures that await sinners, Markandeya worshipped the feet of Nandikesvara again and enquired about the expiatory rites for these sins.

# Rites to be performed in Arunachala for Expiation of Sins

Nandikesvara said to Markandeya:

I shall describe fully the expiatory rites for sins. Listen carefully. The murderer of a *brahmin* should come to Sonadri, bathe in the *Khadga Tirtha*, smear sacred ash and wear *rudraksha*, repeat the *Panchakshara*, worship Paramesvara with devotion and fasting, beg his food for a period of one year, feed *brahmins* and control his senses. If he does so, the sin of murdering a *brahmin* will be expiated and he will attain the world of Brahma.

He who has taken an intoxicating drink should spend one year at Arunachala in the manner prescribed above, worship Mahesvara and pour milk over the *Linga* while chanting *Sata Rudram*. He will then be absolved of his sin. If the stealer of gold, worships Hara at Arunachala with *bilva* leaves and feeds *brahmins* he will be free of his sin. The paramour of the *Guru's* wife should live at Arunachala in like manner and in addition should light a thousand lamps on the ascension of the *Krittika* star, worship Isa for three months, conduct marriage of a learned and poor *brahmin* and repeat the *Panchakshara* a hundred times. He will then be rid of his sin. He will also abide in the world of Siva until he attains Liberation. The lover of other men's wives should stay at Arunachala with his senses under control, worship the Lord of Arunachala with flowers for a month. He will then be free of his sin.

If the poisoner and the slanderer stay at Aruna, leading an austere life as stated above and offer milk to the Lord and teach the Vedas, they will be freed of their sins. The incendiary should dwell at Arunachala for three months leading an austere life, build a house and give it free to a devotee of Siva. The despiser of *dharma* should abide here, build wayside inns for pilgrims according to his ability and make arrangements to feed the pilgrims. One who has betrayed his parents should live here for one month and make gifts of thousands of cows to the Lord and *brahmin*s and feed many a *brahmin* during the solar and lunar eclipses. The murderer of a woman or a child should make gifts of gingelly seeds to *brahmins* and chant hymns to *Isvara* in the prescribed manner.

Let him who has polluted wells and tanks dig wells and tanks at this place. Let him who has misappropriated the lands of others endow lands to the Lord of Arunadri at this place. Let him who has destroyed gardens create parks for Him. Let him who has deprived another of his house construct *mantapas* for the Lord. He who has wronged another should offer money to the Lord of Arunachala and propitiate Him. His sin will then be expiated. He will definitely attain the higher worlds. He who has taken meat should stay here for three fortnights and worship the Lord of Arunachala with offerings and repeat His name. Seekers after Liberation should stay at Aruna, worship the Lord, repeat the *Arunesa mantra* and circumambulate the Hill. Men of wisdom utter the name of Arunachala, whenever they happen to rejoice or experience a nightmare, sneeze, stumble, fall down or commit an error.

He who has been ostracised, and he who is a traitor to Siva becomes sinless by merely staying at Arunachala for three days. This is the world of Siva on earth. It is the form adopted by the Lord praised as *Vedasiras* i.e., the crest of the Vedas. One attains the goal of life at other places through austerities, but here one attains it the moment one thinks of Arunachala. Understand that religious acts performed here have greater efficacy than those performed on the banks of the Ganga, at Prayaga, at Kasi, at Sethu, at Pushkaram or at any other sacred place. Therefore *Agnishtoma*, *Vajapeya*, *Vairaja*, *Sarvatomukha*, *Rajasuya*, *Asvamedha* and *Soma* (names of various kinds of *yagas*) should all be performed at Arunachala.

Fasting for a day at Arunachala is more beneficial than observing a hundred *chandrayanas* (regulated and restricted intake of food) or *santapanas* (living upon the five products of the cow[1] for five days, taking only one product a day, taking water alone on the sixth and fasting completely on the seventh day) elsewhere. The great gifts (*mahadanas*) made here are sixteen times as efficacious as offered at other places. Religious acts prescribed in the *kalpas* which are performed here are twice as efficacious.

On learning these details from Nandikesvara, Markandeya prostrated and asked him about the articles to be offered to Arunachaleswara on particular days, particular seasons etc.

---

[1] The five products of the cow are milk, curds, ghee, its urine and dung. These are considered sacred in the Hindu religion.

# IV. Offerings to Arunachala

NANDIKESVARA said to Markandeya: If one worships the Lord of Aruna with red flowers on Sunday he will prosper and gain sovereignty. He who worships with the *kasturi pachai* leaves on Monday will attain *satyaloka*. Worshipping of the Lord with white lotuses on Thursday results in the worshipper reaching *jnanaloka*. If one worships Arunachala on Friday with *champaka* and jasmine flowers one will reach *tapoloka* and he who worships with *jatimalli* on Saturday will never enter hell even if he be the greatest sinner on earth.

If one offers to the Lord *payasa* (rice pudding) on *prathama* (the first day of the waxing/waning moon) one will acquire wealth and grains and pulses in plenty. The offer of cooked rice and curds on *dvitiya* (the second day) will make one fortunate and gain eminence. If one offers *vadai* (round fried cake made of pulses) on *tritiya* (the third day) one will be healthy and free from disease. If it is offered on *chaturthi* (the fourth day) one will obtain grains in plenty and his desires will be fulfilled. *Ven pongal* (a preparation of rice with pulse, etc.) offered on *panchami* (the fifth day) results in continued prosperity. If one offers *sarkarai pongal* (a preparation of rice cooked with jaggery, etc.) on *sashti* (the sixth day) he is rewarded with the birth of sons. If one offers *ellannam* (cooked rice flavoured with sesame) on *saptami* (the seventh day) one will be freed from debts. The offer of *rajasali chennel anna* (rice of a superior variety) on *ashtami* (the eighth day) bestows power to influence even kings. The offer of a wheat dish on *navami* (the ninth day) makes one free from consumption. *Kadambam* (rice cooked with a variety of vegetables) offered on *dasami* (the tenth day) leads to eternal happiness. *Aval* (beaten rice) offered on *ekadasi* (the eleventh day) makes one free from fear. If cooked rice and pulses are offered on *dwadasi* (the twelfth day) one's desires get fulfilled. *Sattumavu* (wheat flour mixed with jaggery) offered on *trayodasi* (the thirteenth day) makes one free from sorrow and gives peace of mind. By offering various kinds of fruits on *chaturdasi* (the fourteenth day) even a man of dull intellect becomes wise. The offer of jack-fruit on *pournami* (the full-moon day) heals eye-diseases. The offer of edible roots and tubers on *amavasya* (the new-moon day) satisfies one's manes (*pitris*).

Clothes should be offered to Lord Arunachala with devotion on the ascension of the star *Asvini*; ornaments on

*Bharani*; lighted lamps on *Krittika*; silver on *Rohini*; sandal paste on *Mrigasirsha*; *hari chandana* (a special kind of sandal paste) on *Arudra*; civet on *Punarvasu*; scented camphor on *Pushya*; saffron on *Aslesha*; water of the Ganga on *Makha*; betel leaves and arecanuts on *Purva Phalguna*; incense on *Uttara Phalguna*; *agaru* (*agallochum*) on *Hastha*; scented sandal paste on *Chitra*; fragrant *vrinda* flowers on *Svati*; fly whisks on *Visakha*; a white umbrella on *Anuradha*; cows on *Jyeshta*; strings of pearls on *Moola*; a crown on *Purvaashada*; jewels on *Uttaraashada*; a pedestal on *Sravana*; gold on *Sravishta*; clothes on *Satabhishak*; various objects of luxury on *Purva Bhadrapada*; horses on *Uttara Bhadrapada*; a golden chariot on *Revati*. These should be offered after first worshipping the Lord of Arunachala in an elaborate manner. On the days on which the sun enters Aries and the other signs of the zodiac, *Panchamrita* (five sweet ingredients made into a paste) should be poured over the Lord morning and evening. Camomile (*Maruthonri*), *nochi*, *kadambam*, *veppilai*, *padiri*, jasmine, lotus, sweet marjoram, *nandiyavattai* and water lily should then be offered chanting *Siva Panchakshara* all the time. On the days of the winter and summer solstices, *panchakavya* should be poured on the *Linga* while chanting *Shadakshara mantra* and milk should be poured to the accompaniment of chanting of *Pranava* (*i.e.*, *OM*). Afterwards the Lord should be adorned with *rudra tulasi* in the morning, *malaka* at noon and jasmine in the evening.

At the time of *Ardhodaya* (rising of the half moon) a thousand pots of pure water should be poured over the

*Linga* while chanting the *Sata Rudra Stotra*. Aspirants for Liberation should keep vigil on *Sivaratri*. They should on that day worship the Lord of Arunachala with the *bilva* leaves and lotus to the accompaniment of drums and cymbals and singing and dancing.

In the month of *Pushya* the *Agneya* festival should be celebrated along with chanting the *vyabritis* (primal sounds, namely, *bhuh*, *bhuvah*, *suvah*) and the offer of rice and vegetable dishes. In the month of *Vaisaka* the *Damanaka* festival should be celebrated according to the *agamas* of Siva. In the month of *Margasira* (December-January) the Lord should be worshipped early in the morning with *puja* and *abhishekam* with the chanting of *Sama Veda*. On Saturdays, the evenings of *Trayodasi* (the thirteenth day of the waning/waxing moon), the *Arudra Vyatipata* (a sacred day), the days of eclipse, and Sundays and Mondays, special worship should be offered according to the *agamas*.

A wise man will worship the Lord of Arunachala on the day he takes *diksha* (consecration for a religious ceremony), when he has *upanayana* (the ceremonial wearing of the sacred thread) performed and when he celebrates a marriage or the birth of a son. The Lord of Arunachala should be worshipped with flowers when religious vows are observed, or when buildings are constructed or when one suddenly gains fortune or when one is going to war. If one is at a great distance from Arunachala one should think of it always, if one lives nearby one should have *darshan* of it and if one is living inside the temple one should worship the Lord morning, noon and evening.

Child! What more do you want? There is none expect Arunachala to grant Heaven and Liberation. The mind becomes pure by thinking of Arunachala, the ears by hearing His name, the eyes by seeing Him and the tongue by uttering His Name. Those who are born at Arunachala enjoy all happiness and attain Liberation on death. If *sraddha* (a ceremony to propitiate the manes) is performed here, they too will attain Liberation. This Arunachala is superior to the seven centres which grants Liberation viz., Ayodhya, Mathura, Maya, Kanchi, Kasi, Avantika and Dvaraka.

# V. Creation Described

NANDIKESVARA said: O Markandeya! It is indeed a hard task to narrate the glory of Arunachala. Nevertheless I shall do so. You are one of the foremost devotees of Siva and eager to hear all about Him. A man who does not know about the greatness of Arunachala is but an animal. Even if one knows it, how can one describe it? The legend of the Lord of Sonachala is the glory of Sambhu. It brings good fortune to him who hears it. The glory of Arunachala is so great that even the wise and the intelligent cannot comprehend its true significance even if they hear it times without number. When I think of Siva's divine play my mind is filled with sublime bliss and I am overwhelmed. Nevertheless I shall narrate the enchanting story of Arunachala.

In the beginning, i.e. at the commencement of the age of the *devas* (*devakalpa*), Mahesvara the immutable Lord had a desire to create the universe. The three-eyed Siva brought forth Brahma from his right side and Vishnu from his left. He endowed Brahma with the quality of *rajas* and Vishnu with *sattva* and entrusted them with the task of creation and sustenance of the universe respectively.

Brahma created out of his mind ten noble sons, the first of whom was Marichi, and out of his thumb Daksha Prajapati and made them carry on the task of creation. To Kashyapa, the son of Marichi, were born the *suras*, the *asuras*, the *marut-ganas*, the eagles, the *gandharvas* and the *apsaras*. Human beings are the progeny of Manu. To Atri were born *rishis*, *brahmin*s and *kshatriyas*. *Yakshas* and *rakshasas* were born to Pulaha and Pulastya — Udatya and Brihaspati to the Muni Angiras and Agni to Bhrigu; Chyavana and Vasishta and other *Maharshis* were the sons of Bhrigu.

Thus, the world was filled with the progeny of Brahma. As a result of this, after some time, he forgot Maheswara, his Creator. Vishnu's consort was Kamala, daughter of Bhrigu. He incarnated on earth as a fish and in other forms, and in due course forgot *Isvara*, his Lord. Thus Brahma and Vishnu forgetting Siva became proud and arrogant thinking that there was none superior to them.

When arrogance and pride entered their minds there arose a dispute between Brahma and Vishnu each of whom considered himself the Supreme Lord. Brahma, the creator of the world, (on account of the excess of *rajas* in him) became bluish in complexion and said to Vishnu: "Why are you under the delusion that you are greater than I, for am I not the creator of the world and therefore the father of creation? You are deluded by your pride at having killed Madhu and Kaitabha who came out of you. As you are full of *tamas* (darkness) how can there be any *sattva* (light) at all in you? Do you realize that you are dull by nature on account of your prolonged sleep. Janardana! How can the three worlds under my control be said to be protected by you, hiding as you do in the sea for fear of *asuras*? The four Vedas have come out of my four mouths. Saraswati who is Pure Consciousness is my spouse. The animate and inanimate beings, in all the three worlds were created by me. They are sustained by Indra and other *devatas* who are but my sons and grandsons. Can anyone be superior to me, the Creator and Lord, of all the worlds?"

When Brahma uttered these harsh words, in a fit of anger and jealousy, Narayana replied scornfully: "Brahma! Do not in anger shout in vain. Remember that you came out of the lotus which sprang up from my navel. If I had not woken up from my *yogic* sleep and slain Madhu and Kaitabha you would have lost your life long ago at their hands. Of my own accord, with the object of killing Somaka and other *daityas* and saving the Vedas and *dharma* I took many incarnations. Therefore, who except myself is the source and mover of all creation? Those who are full of *rajas* cannot discern anything clearly. You are full of *rajas*. Goddess Lakshmi who dwells in the lotus is my spouse. How can the elements, time and the ego of the

Self, appear in the three worlds without me, the substratum of all? The *adityas*, *vasus*, *rudras*, *dikpalakas* and *manus* are all myself. Know that the three *vyahrtis* and the *Vedas* are my manifestations. The power of creation pertains to me. How can you be superior than or even equal to me. Know that I am the Lord of the three worlds."

Steeped in sheer ignorance Brahma and Vishnu continued their wordy duel and soon they entered into a terrible rage. The Sun, the Moon, stars and planets did not rise and set, the five elements became extinct and the very existence of the universe was threatened. Indra and the other *devas*, the protectors of the quarters and the *Maharshis* thought that the end of the world (*kalpantam*) would soon follow. On account of this great calamity all living beings were put to great distress. The Lord of all beings saw that darkness had overpowered the universe. As he was the Lord of the universe he wished to save it. He perceived the delusion that had overcome Brahma and Vishnu. He thought thus: "Both of them have forgotten me their Lord and, in their arrogance, each is considering himself the Lord. Both of them are deluded. Ah! How strange is the power of delusion! These two, Brahma and Vishnu, have come to this plight due to their ego. Men who have lost their wisdom are enveloped by the darkness of ignorance. Now I shall make them realize their folly."

Taking pity on His children, the compassionate Lord Mahesa decided to rid them of their ego-sense. Boundless indeed is the compassion of the Lord who wears the crescent moon! It is His very nature. It radiates, blessing all the three worlds. His grace flows everywhere. Later, Brahma and Vishnu both became free of their ego on account of His infinite grace.

# VI. The Appearance of an Effulgent *Linga* Before Brahma and Vishnu

MARKANDEYA asked Nandikesvara: Lord! Kindly tell me how Sambhu saved Brahma and Vishnu from their delusion? Nandikesvara replied, "I shall describe how Siva, saviour of His devotees showered His Grace upon Brahma and Vishnu."

"Before them, there arose suddenly a Column of Effulgence which pierced the sky, pervading the universe. And the deep blue sky was made invisible by the dazzle of this Column which seemed to suddenly shoot out of the *Brahmanda* (i.e. cosmos). There was a sudden blaze in all the directions. The seas appeared to have been devoured by the immense tongue of the flame. The oceans on the earth became still as though they had regained their true nature. Stars and planets shining in the sky looked like sparks emitted by the Column of Effulgence. The intergalactic space appeared to be covered with a red glow. There was only the brightness of the Column dominating the entire space and nothing else. The earth appeared to be covered with vermilion (*kumkum*) and the quarters appeared to be strewn with *sindura* (an ochre coloured powder). The sky looked red everywhere. The vault of heaven shone with a red glow. All things in the world, moving and stationary, appeared to be red reflected by the glow of the Column of Effulgence.

On seeing this dazzling Column of Fire the four-faced Brahma and the four-armed Vishnu were wonderstruck, and forgetting their altercation reflected thus: 'What a strange and brilliant Column of Fire? Have the twelve *Adityas* (Suns) risen together between the earth and the sky to bring about the end of the *kalpa* (aeon)? It has dulled our vision by its glow and has grown so large that nothing else can be perceived. Although it blazes fiercely it emits no heat. It does not, like fire, burn even objects that are close by. By being exposed to its light not only the world but our frames too have become red. Whence and how has this risen? Where is its source? How did it grow so large? For what purpose and by what power does it shine? What are its limits? It spreads above, below and in all directions. The mind desires to delve into *patala* (nether world), or fly up in the sky to see how far it extends.'

Both Brahma and Vishnu were agitated in this manner when they saw the Column of Effulgence. Vishnu said smilingly to the extremely proud Brahma, 'Son! This is a touchstone which has made its appearance to test both of us who claimed superiority. Neither of us can discover the limits of this column which undoubtedly is of immeasurable glory. Therefore, without trying to do so we shall regard as superior he who between us finds out either its beginning or its end. He alone is the Lord of the World.' Brahma agreed. Each became eager to discover either the beginning or the end of that Column of Effulgence.

## Vishnu Seeks the Origin of the Column

Nandikesvara continued:

Brahma took the form of a swan and started on his quest saying, 'I shall discover the top of this Column'. Vishnu took the form of a boar capable of digging and penetrating the earth and eagerly began his search for the bottom of the Column of Effulgence. When that huge boar bristled up, ploughed the earth with its horns and cleft it with its snout, it looked as if it were paying its obeisance to the Column of Light. It grunted in excitement over the hard task as it entered *patala* swiftly. But however far that god in the form of a boar penetrated, he saw the Column extending further. Numerous serpents rose from the clefts of the earth like tongues of flame rising from the pillar of fire. Achyuta (Vishnu) saw that the ancient tortoise supporting the earth looked like a part of the Column of Fire. He saw the elephants of the quarters standing far apart beneath the earth, each carrying his burden, swaying gently. Vishnu espied also the primal power (*adharasakhi*) by the grace of which Sesha (the serpent), Kurma (the tortoise) and others bear the weight of the earth. The lotus eyed god (Vishnu) traversed with difficulty the seven *patalas* (nether worlds) named *Atala*, *Vitala*, *Sutala*, *Talatala*, *Rasatala*, *Mahatala* and *Patala* and the denizens dwelling in these worlds and reached the city of Bhagavati belonging to Virochana. He also traversed the other realms of *daityas* saying, 'This I have passed, this I have crossed' and penetrated further and further down. Madhava's aim was to discover the origin of the column. Even when he had reached the bottom of the ocean of milk (*kshirasagara*) he saw the Column of Effulgence extending further down. Although he had crossed hundreds of nether worlds the foot of the Column of Effulgence was nowhere in sight. Even after the lapse of a thousand years its origin could not be discovered by the boar. The boar became extremely weary; its body was tired, its face injured and it became breathless. It could not take one step further. Thus humbled, his pride and arrogance destroyed, Vishnu realised that however much he tried he would never be able to reach the bottom of the Coloum of Fire. Vishnu now turned back although his desire had not been fulfilled. To him who was now full of humility, the very Column of Brightness became a beacon to lead his way back to earth from the nether world. As he rose from the nether region, again traversing many worlds, Vishnu was profusely perspiring. At last he reached Arunachala with great difficulty. It looked as if he had been bound by the force of the Column of Effulgence. He said to himself: 'Just as I could not discover the bottom of this mass of Effulgence, even so the Creator (Brahma) cannot discover its top. Leaving the quest aside I shall surrender myself to Siva, the Lord from whom this mass of Effulgence has originated. It is He who has pervaded the world and the regions beyond it. These troubles arose simply because I had been deluded by ignorance and had forgotten Him.'

After coming to this decision Vishnu abandoned his pride and reached the place where the Column of Effulgence stood steady.

## Brahma Seeks the Top of the Column of Effulgence

Nandikesvara continued:

As for Brahma, he flew up swiftly in the form of a swan and followed the Column of Effulgence. Initially, by the force of its wings the swan waded through all obstacles. As he soared higher the earth became invisible and looked like a small dot in space. The speed of the swan surpassed all ethereal velocities. However high and hard he flew he still saw the Column of Effulgence extending further up. Even after traversing the region of the seven *Maruts* he saw it piercing the firmament of heaven and blazing upwards and even beyond it. He wondered at this and thought as follows:

How can I face Hari without seeing the summit? What is the use of prolonging this life which has not seen the fulfilment of its desire? What is it that is going to be accomplished by this life of mine? What will be my fate? If I deceive Vishnu how will he come to know of it? When the opponent cannot be conquered by straightforward means, he should be defeated by deceit. For, is not honour one's precious wealth?

While Brahma thought thus and felt miserable, he saw a white streak approach him. Even as he wondered as to what it was, it came near and he saw that it was a flower of the screw-pine. Though faded, it was very fragrant and pure. Brahma took it in his hands, whereupon the flower spoke to him, "Ah! Why do you stop me? I have been travelling for many thousands of years and am tired. Please let me go."

At this Brahma looked again at the Column of Effulgence and overcome by fatigue, reflected thus, "One who does not keep his word is worthless. What is the significance of this Effulgence which pervades the earth and sky? My wings are almost broken, my eyes blind and my limbs weary. I am about to fall down. Why should I speak more? It looks as if my life-breath is leaving me. Let the thick knot of the ego be severed. Let my rivalry with Mukunda (Vishnu) come to an end at once. This mass of Effulgence extends beyond the open sky and still remains as it was before! Neither I nor Narayana (Vishnu) can understand this. I have no strength to proceed further. Nor am I able to return." Thinking and wondering within himself thus, Brahma turned to the flower and asked, "Who are you? Where are you coming from?" It replied, "I am a flower of the screw-pine. I am sentient. I dwelt on the crest of this column for a long time at Siva's command. I am now coming down as I desire to see the world."

On hearing this Brahma was slightly relieved. He asked the flower, "How far away is the top of this Column of Effulgence?"

## Brahma Requests the Screw-pine Flower to Bear False Witness

Nandikesvara continued:

The flower of the screw-pine derisively smiled at Brahma and said: "Who are you? You seem to know nothing. You cannot know the origin of this column. There are crores and crores of *Brahmandas* inside this column. They are countless. Who can measure its dimensions? I have been coming down for many thousands of four-fold *yugas* (*Chatur-yugas*). Yet I have not perceived the earth which is its middle region." When Brahma heard this he abandoned his pride, clasped his hands, bowed to it and prayed:

"O great soul in the form of a flower of the screw-pine! I am Brahma, the Creator. There arose a dispute between Vishnu and myself. Both of us forgot the glory of Siva. We became proud of our work, creating and sustaining the world. It is said that friendship arises even by exchanging seven words (*sneham saptapadam*). You are a great soul. You must forgive my ignorance and be gracious to me. We began seeking the top and bottom of this

Column of Effulgence in order to establish superiority over each other. Vishnu took the form of a boar and I, that of a swan. I am unaware of Vishnu's fate. I who came to find the summit have flown for thousands of years and become weary. My life seems to be ebbing. Friend! Fortunately I have met you. I am helpless. You are now my saviour. Pray, grant my wish. I beseech you. If Vishnu has seen the bottom of this column, I am defeated. If he has not seen it, I am equal to him. Either way it would be a disgrace. Friend! You alone can now retrieve me from this predicament. You must utter a lie for me, your friend. Kindly avow in the presence of Vishnu that I have seen the summit of the Column of Effulgence and that you were witness to it since you (the flower) always decorate Siva's head. Further, declare that I (Brahma) am superior to Vishnu."

Implored thus, the screw-pine swore in the presence of the Column of Effulgence that Brahma had reached the summit.

# VII. SANKARA EMERGES FROM THE COLUMN OF EFFULGENCE

NANDIKESVARA continued: Vishnu looked at Brahma in disbelief. He was certain that Brahma had not reached the summit of the Column. He laughed and thought, "Only the Deva of *devas*, the Lord of all beings, can bless me who am under a delusion and can humble the pride of Brahma. He humbled me who in my pride tried to discover the bottom of the column of *jyoti*. And so my devotion poured forth for Tryambaka (the three-eyed God) the *Svayambhu* (Self-originated). Being devoid of ego-sense I shall praise the Supreme Lord. The two of us originated from Him. Brahma, in his pride, still deceives me with perjury. Siva, the destroyer of sorrow is my only refuge. Who but Him can save me, one who am guilty and disloyal to his Lord and Master? Therefore I shall praise my Lord."

Reflecting thus, Vishnu praised Siva as follows, "Hail! Thou who art in the form of earth, water, fire, air, and Hota (one who makes the oblations in the fire)! Hail! Thou who art in the form of *akasa* (ether)! Thou who transcendest the three *gunas*! Save me. Thou who art in the form of Time! Save me. Thou who dost possess imperishable wealth! Save me. Ocean of compassion! redeem me. Thou art the creator of all, the protector of all and the destroyer of all. Who is there apart from Thee? Thou art smaller than the smallest (atom) and greater than the greatest. Thou pervadest everything inside and out. The *Vedas* are Thy breath. The universe reveals Thy glorious creation. Thou art That. Thou art all that belongs to Thee. You are the very embodiment of knowledge. *Devas*, *danavas*, *daityas*, *siddhas*, *vidyadharas*, human beings, animals, birds, mountains, trees are all Thy form. Thou art both *naraka* (hell) and *Svarga* (heaven). Thou art the Goal of life. Thou art *Yoga*. Lord! What is there which is not Thyself? Thou art the beginning, middle and end of all animate and inanimate beings. Thou abidest in all in the form of Time. Thou art Siva, the Supreme Lord, the controller of destinies of *jivas*, He who blesses all."

Vishnu next said to himself, "Siva should, by some means or other, be directly perceived by me. By seeing Him and surrendering to Him I shall attain Liberation. If I cannot perceive Him I shall praise His abode as well as I can. He who is capable of hearing all will hear this too and bestow His grace on me" and began to praise Siva thus, "Hail! Deva! Mahadeva! Vamadeva! Vrishadhwaja (he who has the emblem of the bull on his banner)! Kalantaka (Slayer of *Kala*, Time)! Yajnanasaka (the destroyer of the sacrifice)! Nilakantha (the blue-throated one)! Chandrasekhara (the wearer of the crescent moon)! Hail Sambhu (home of everything good)! Siva (Auspicious one)! Isana (the Ruler)! Sarva (All)! Tryambaka (three-eyed one)! Dhurjati (one who has matted locks)! Kamari (the foe of Kama, the God of desire)! Purari (the enemy of the three cities)! Sthanu (the motionless being)! Bhava (the truly existent one)! Mahesvara (the great Lord)! Hail! Isa (Ruler)! Sali (the bearer of the trident)! Pasupati (the Lord of *jivas*)! Hara (Destroyer of sin)! Sarvajna Jyoti (the all-knowing effulgence)! Bhutesa! Bhutadhipa! (Lord of all beings)! Kapali (the bearer of the skull)! Nilanetra (the blue eyed one)! Hail! Rudra! Pinaki (the wearer of the bow named Pinaka)! Gangadhara (the wearer of Ganga)! Vyamakesa (he whose locks spread in space)! Girisa (the Lord of the mountains)! Parameswara (the Supreme Lord)! Hail! Bhima (the mighty one)! Thou who disguisest thyself as a hunter! Repository of compassion! Krishnuretah (one whose seed fell into the fire)! Kailasapati (Lord of Kailasa)! At Thy behest the wind blows, Adishesha (the great serpent) supports the earth, the sun and moon shine and the *Brahmanda,* i.e., cosmos exists as vast expanse of space. It is at Thy command that the bright constellations move in the heavens. By Thy Grace, Brahma and I continue to create and sustain the universe. Thou causest the earth to produce nourishing crops and holdest the seas within their bounds. The supernatural powers like *anima* (shrinking to an atom) are very insignificant for Thee. How can I ignore Thee who art praised by all the other *amaras* (immortal ones)? We think of Thee only in times of need. But Thou shouldst not, on that account, become displeased with Thy devotees. Thou shouldst always be merciful to them. Devotion to Thee is wisdom. When Thou concealest it, there is delusion. These are the causes of bondage and liberation."

When Chakrapani (Vishnu, the Wielder of the Wheel) humbly folded his hands and praised Siva, Padmasambhava (lotus-born), Brahma scorned him. Immediately Pasupati Siva, manifested himself before them.

## Brahma Praises Siva

Nandikesvara continued:

Splitting asunder the column of light, Siva appeared before the two (Brahma and Vishnu). He was like the full-moon, was mounted on a bull which was white like the peak of Kailash, was wearing matted locks and the crescent moon on his head, a garland of skulls on his neck, a serpent in the place of the sacred thread, serpents for earrings, and with an eye on his forehead, five faces and five long curved blue throats. He carried in his hands, the trident, the skull, the tiny drum (*damaru*), the deer, the axe, the bow, the *khatvanga* (a staff with a skull at the top), the sword and two serpents, one on each side. His body was whitish, he wore a lower garment of tiger skin and an upper garment of elephant hide. Thus majestically adorned He was praised by all the *devas*.

When the lotus-eyed Vishnu saw him, he danced with joy. The guilty Brahma on seeing the Lord's true form was confused and frightened. Mahadeva looked graciously at Madhava (Vishnu) while with a 'Humkar' expressed His anger at Brahma's falsehood. He then said, "The two of you need not be ashamed for having transcended your limits. Hari (Vishnu) pondered deeply and became enlightened. But Brahma, on the contrary, has uttered falsehood and I now cut off his fifth head for that perjury. Brahma shall not hereafter be installed in any temple. And this screw-pine flower, which bore false witness, shall never again find a place on my head and shall not be used for my worship."

After cursing Brahma and the screw-pine flower thus, Siva turned to Vishnu and said, "Child! Be composed, I am pleased with you. You are one of my foremost devotees. You originated from me and are my *sattvic* part. At the end of the *kalpa* you shall merge in me."

# VIII. Brahma and Vishnu Erect a Temple for Arunachala

WHEN the three-eyed God blessed thus the devoted and egoless Vishnu, the crestfallen Brahma began to pray.

Brahma addressed Siva thus, "God of gods! Thy glory can be realized only by those who are fortunate enough to obtain Thy grace. Myself, Vishnu and the guardians of the quarters pale into insignificance before Thee the true Lord. Thou alone canst put us in bondage (*pasa*) and release us as well. Having manifested thyself as the fundamental elements, Thou pervadest all. Can even the most learned man discover Thy real nature? Mahadeva! As a hunter surrounded by hounds, Thou, with the Vedas, huntest relentlessly and slayest the beasts known as lust, anger, greed, delusion, pride and envy.

"Why recall the punishment which Virabhadra at Thy command meted out to Thine enemies at the sacrifice performed by Daksha? Thy intellect (*buddhi*) which is the time-consuming fire (*kalagni*) can burn up the entire universe. It does not permit Manmatha, the god of love, to shoot his arrows of flowers at Thee. The guilty Jalandhara was torn asunder by Thy trident. The god of death and the other demons were annihilated by Thee. Who can oppose Thee? Could we have remained alive now if Thou hadst not swallowed the *alakaala* poison? In ancient times Thou didst awaken from their sleep of ignorance the recluses of the *daruka* forest who were staunch upholders of the *Vedic* rites and, appearing before them in disguise, didst bless them graciously. If Thou hadst not crushed beneath Thy big toe the most cruel Apasmara (the demon of forgetfulness), the entire world would have been plunged into darkness. If Thou were not partly man and partly woman, how could I have created this world of moving and stationary beings? O Sambhu! For what length of time did the arm of Sambara, which Thy anger had paralysed, stay uplifted as Thy pillar of victory! Consider how Vishnu pierced himself with a spear and became stupefied when he tried to fill with his blood the skull which Thou didst carry about like a beggar. If Thou hadst not taught Parasurama the use of various weapons and missiles, how could he, however wrathful, have offerred oblations of blood for the satisfaction of the souls of his ancestors? If Thou hadst not, in the form of a *sarabha*, subdued Narasimha he would have joined hands with Hiranyakasipu and destroyed the entire world. Thou didst, in the guise of a fisherman, draw the fish and the tortoise in the ocean of *kalpa*. Thou didst bind Vishnu with serpent ropes in the form of Narasimha and the boar. When Vishnu wished to worship Thee with a thousand flowers and found one short he plucked out one of his lotus-eyes and offerred it to you as the thousandth. Thou gavest him, as a reward for this act, the discus (*chakra*) called Sudarsana with which he overcame the *daityas*."

Nandikesvara continued:

When Brahma praised Siva thus and Vishnu also implored Him on Brahma's behalf, Siva took pity on Brahma and restored to him the role of Creator. He also ordained that Brahma be worshipped at *yajnas*, *yagas* and *homas* (*Vedic* sacrifices). He looked at Brahma and Vishnu lovingly and said, "Neither of you should henceforth forget me and become arrogant. Carry on vigilantly your work of creation and sustenance without forgetting me. Let this sacred Arunachala which has been blessed by me for your sake become a place where men can attain liberation. I ordain that those who live within a distance of three *yojanas* (about thirty miles) of this place shall become one with me even without initiation or spiritual practices. Those lowly creatures which move about and those that are stationary will get liberated by simply living here. Those who see me or even remember me irrespective of where they may live, will realise the essence of *Vedanta*, otherwise very difficult to acquire. My effulgent form will shine here forever as eternal immutable Arunachala. Oceans will not submerge it even at the time of the great deluge. The winds will not shake it and the world-destroying fire will not burn it. The bright constellations of stars will perpetually go round this *Linga* of Effulgence. Every being blessed by me will not only be born here but will also, after death, attain liberation. Even sinners who bow down to this hill from a distance or come near and circumambulate it will attain liberation. Great souls alone live here. One cannot attain liberation at any other place. Therefore never leave this place."

On hearing these words of Kamari (the enemy of *Kama*, the god of love) Brahma and Vishnu humbly bowed down to Siva and prayed:

"Sustainer of the universe! Let this Hill be the mainstay of the world as stated by you. But, moderate its effulgence, O Rudra, so that it becomes bearable, yet retains its boundless glory and remains a repository of everything auspicious. But let it reveal, for the world's welfare, its true effulgence once a year in the month of *Kartikai* (November-December) on the evening of the full moon in the asterism of *Krittika.* Mahadeva! Although this Red Hill exists for the welfare of all, none could worship it without Thy grace. The God of gods should, therefore, graciously respond to our prayer and abide here forever in the form of a *Linga*. We can then worship it in the prescribed manner with ablutions, sandal paste, flowers and other offerings. There are ever so many flowering plants and trees at this place. O repository of compassion! Great Lord! If Thou graciously abidest here we shall worship and meditate upon Thee and our devotion to Thee will become steady. Only thus would our minds become pure. Thou shouldst, therefore, abide with love as a *Sivalinga* on the eastern side of this Hill so that we may, by Thy grace, get rid of our primal nescience. It is Thou who didst manifest as the Vedas, the *vedangas*, the *dharma sastras*, the *puranas*, and the *agamas* and didst teach them to others. Thou must, therefore, abide here in the form of a *Guru* so that both of us as well as devotees may attain liberation. Sankara! There are the twenty-eight *Siva agamas*. How, according to them, shall we meditate upon Thee and when shall we get rid of this delusion that arose out of ignorance?"

After praying thus, Brahma and Vishnu touched Siva's lotus-feet with reverence. At this the Lord of Parvati looked at them and said, "O children! You have spoken properly. The same thought occurred to me. Both of you may worship me taking as guidance the *kamika agamas*. You seem to have, in your confusion, forgotten certain *samhitas*. You will now, by my grace, recollect them."

After instructing Brahma and Vishnu thus, Siva disappeared from their view and an auspicious *Sivalinga* appeared instead. Brahma and Vishnu looked at it in wonder and made their obeisance to it with great joy. Next, they ordered Visvakarma to erect a temple for Arunachaleswara. They created, for the *abhisheka* of the Lord, a *tirtha* (a sacred tank) containing the waters of all the holy *tirthas*. They also founded a city nearby and named it Arunachala.

Those who visit Arunachala do not care for any other achievement. Even Siva abiding there does not care for

Kailasa. *Devas*, *gandharvas*, *vidyadharas*, *yakshas*, *apsaras*, *siddhas* and *Brahmarshis* choose to live there. Ganga and the other *tirthas* abide there in the form of wells and tanks, the *Nandana* (the garden of Indra) in the form of forests and parks, the *Gokula* of Sri Krishna in the form of herds of cows, the Vedas in the form of the *agama* scriptures, mountains in the form of *gopuras* (temple towers), the *smritis* in the form of religious injunctions and *bhutas*, *pretas*, *pisachas* and *vetalas* (denizens of the spirit-world) in human form. Siva Himself abides here forever as a *siddha purusha* known as Arunagiri Yogi wearing only a loin-cloth (*kaupina*) and with matted locks and forehead shining with marks of *vibhuti.* Vishnu and other lords of the worlds, worship the Lord of Arunachala here. They act as *acharyas* and guide the aspirants in the worship of the Lord. Even Brahma and Vishnu pay their obeisance to the Lord as prescribed in the *agamas*.

I have thus fully revealed to you the secrets which I learned from the wise. Nandikesvara concluded, what more do you wish to know?

# IX. The Union of Siva and Parvati

SUTA said to the *rishis*: When Nandikesvara asked Markandeya whether he wished to know anything more, the latter replied, "Deva of *devas!* We have heard from you what has to be heard. Still I and the *rishis* are eager to know about Goddess Parvati's *tapas* here and how She won the left half of Siva."

Upon this, Nandikesvara said: Oh Sage Markandeya! Listen attentively. I shall now narrate the events leading to Parvati's arrival and Her austerities at Arunachala.

You know that the Supreme Lord had earlier married Sati, the daughter of Daksha. You also know that when Daksha insulted Her Lord during the *yaga* performed by the former, She flew into a rage and threw herself into the sacrificial fire. You also know how Siva created Virabhadra from His matted locks and commanded him to behead

Daksha along with his cohorts and destroy Daksha's sacrificial fire. He also took to task Brahma, Vishnu, Indra and other gods, and punished the others who stood mute witnesses to the unrighteous act perpetrated by Daksha.

Sati took birth again as the daughter of Himavan (the Himalayas) and acquired the name Himavati, Parvati and later Uma. Once, in the Sthanu forest, Siva was deeply absorbed in *samadhi* and Parvati was serving Him. The *devas,* realising that Siva's *nirguna* state would result in the cessation of all activities in the whole universe, despatched *Kama* (the god of love) with the object of inducing Siva to regain normal waking state. Kama tried to arouse Siva from His *nirvikalpa samadhi* by shooting his cupid arrows at the Lord so that amorous passions may be aroused in Him. But Siva, enraged at the audacity of Kama, burnt him to ashes with his world destroying fire (*Kalagni*). When Parvati found that Siva's wrath had cooled, She proceeded with Her companions to a mountain peak and, by performing austerities, pleased the Lord. Siva then married Her and lived with Her in solitude. Goddess Rati (the wife of Kama) who was mourning the death of Her husband prayed earnestly to Parvati who thereupon performed austerities at Kamapitha and restored him to life. Afterwards Parvati's mother Mena and Her father, the King of the Mountains, took Her to their home. While at Her parents' home, Her thoughts were all the time centred on Siva.

At that time there were two demons (*asuras*) named Sumbha and Nisumbha, who had by the strength of their austerities obtained from Brahma a boon which made them invulnerable to the attacks of *devas*, *asuras* and human beings. The *devas* were afraid of them. They prayed to Siva who comforted them saying, "Fear not. There will be peace in due course. These two demons will be slain." After giving this assurance Siva retired to the inner apartments and continued to dally with Parvati. One day when he was in a mood of endearment he called Her 'Kali' (a dark-skinned woman). At once She cast off Her skin and threw it away. The place where it fell became the holy Kasi. The skin itself turned into a Goddess named Kausiki. This Goddess performed austerities on the Vindhya mountains and, in the course of Her penance killed the two lustful demons. Parvati too performed austerities and succeeded in acquiring a golden complexion. She came to be known as Gowri (fair-complexioned). Siva was pleased with Her. In course of time She gave birth to two sons Ganapati and Subrahmanya. Great souls say that they are Brahma and Vishnu who had been born thus for expiating their sins. The two children, always very active, grew up under the care of their father.

## Parvati Serves the Lord of Aruna

Nandikesvara continued: While Siva and Parvati were thus leading a happy life, Parvati one day saw Siva seated under a mango tree, deeply absorbed. She was assailed with a doubt whether Siva was faithful to Her and whether He was thinking of another woman. She decided to win

His unflinching love. Her thoughts ran in this manner, "I must perform austerities and win his love. Once he opens his eyes he will not let me go. I must leave before he opens them." Resolving thus, She went away without taking leave of Him. She did not stop even when Her companions tried to dissuade Her from going. Thereupon Her five companions Kalavati, Malyavati, Malini, Vijaya and Jaya followed Her.

They wandered over several mountain ranges and forests, visited many sacred *tirthas* and temples and at last reached the Dravida country at the foot of the Sahaya Mountains. They crossed the Pennai river. Parvati then said to Vijaya, "See, there in the distance is Arunagiri. On its slopes are situated *ashrams* of *rishis* who practise austerities. They are powerful and are known for their protective nature. Let us go and have their *darshan* and blessings." Her words aroused the curiosity of Her friends. At this moment Parvati saw an *ashram* on the path leading to the hill, thick with luscious trees. Buffaloes, monkeys, and wild animals roamed about freely. On the banks of the streams and pools used by the sages for their bath, herds of elephants and wild boars were seen. There were also birds, reptiles and rodents. All creatures moved about fearlessly. Smoke from sacrificial fires rose up over the trees. Cuckoos chanted the hymn addressed to God Rudra, crows recited *stotras* (hymns of praise) and parrots sang the Sama Veda. Tigers and cows moved about in friendship.

In such surroundings of peace and perfect harmony, Parvati espied a sage practising austerities in a secluded spot. He was sitting under a *saptaparna* tree on a splendid tiger-skin covered with sacred grass (*darbha*). He was sitting in the posture known as *virasana*. His body was smeared with sacred ash (*vibhuti*) and his hair was red and matted. He was clad in the bark of a tree, had a string of *rudraksha* beads in his hand and was performing *mantra japa*. He looked majestic like an evening cloud over a mountain.

Parvati approached him most reverently and asked him, "O Sage! kindly tell me about this Hill." He replied, "This is Arunachala, the most glorious and sacred place on earth. I am Rishi Gautama and am practising austerities here for attaining liberation." When he learned from Her companions that She was Parvati, he made his obeisance to Her and invited Her to his hermitage and offered Her fruits and honey. He surmised that Parvati was intent on practising austerities for the welfare of the world. He narrated to Her the glory of the Column of Effulgence.

Sage Gautama said to Parvati:

Sambhu always abides at the place known as Sthaleswaram to the east of Sonadri in the form of a *Linga* of Effulgence. I could not perform penance there because Brahma, Vishnu and others visited that place often to pay their homage. I have therefore chosen this place, at the foot of the Hill, as being most suitable for my austerities and have installed a *linga* of the Lord. You too may build a hermitage on the sacred ground near mine and perform your austerities.

The Goddess accordingly built a hermitage there and began Her penance. She appointed Satyavati, Kananavasini,

Subhaga and Dundumari to guard Her hermitage properly in the four directions and the extremely valorous Durga to guard the whole sacred forest where the ascetics resided.

She ceased to adorn herself with ornaments, discarded Her silken robes and changed into one made from the bark of trees and used mat made of coarse *darbha* grass as Her seat. She led a strenuous life by waking up in the early hours of the day, taking bath in the river and walking barefoot upon thorny and stony paths. She propitiated all the gods before beginning worship of Arunachala. She consecrated a *Siva-linga* herself and worshipped it according to the *agamas.*Her austerities consisted of standing motionless like a rock with one pointed attention on Her Lord in the middle of the five fires in summer and in water during the winter. She circumambulated the Arunachala Hill along with Her maids with Her Lord's name ever on the lips and singing His praise. Everyday at Her hermitage, on completion of Her worship, She entertained guests including animals by offering food and drink. The wild animals roamed about Her hermitage freely without harming men or tame animals. She fondly nurtured flower plants, creepers and trees.

With Her kindness, compassion and the spiritual strength gained by Her austerities and devotion to Arunachala She dazzled like a priceless gem in Her coarse garments.

# X. The Goddess Destroys Mahishasura

NANDIKESVARA continued: Mahishasura, the enemy of the *devas*, vanquisher of Indra, conqueror of the worlds, the terror of *siddhas* and *vidyadharas*, the formidable opponent who had obtained a boon which protected him against powerful weapons, was unaffected by spells and was adored by hosts of *asuras* and *rakshasas*. He had slandered the wives of sages. He was an enemy of *dharma* and all that stood for righteousness. He was far stronger than Namuchi and Vritra, and was as powerful as Hiranyaksha of yore.

Mahishasura heard about the Goddess who was doing penance at Arunachala and Her enchanting beauty. He despatched a woman messenger to Her. She approached

Her in the guise of a woman engaged in austerities. She uttered words of cunning and deceit to ensnare the Goddess. She said, "Ah, what is this? You are living in a dreadful forest! You ought to live in the beautiful apartments of a palace. How did the idea of foregoing the pleasures of youth and performing austerities which are difficult even for *devas* occur to you? Instead of sleeping on a bed of swan feathers under a canopy adorned with pearls and jewels, why do you lie on hard rocks? There is none else suitable for you but Mahishasura, the lord of the three worlds who lives close by. If you see him but once you will abandon all your austerities. Well, why should I conceal it from you? That lord, having heard of you, has become enamoured of your beauty and has sent me as messenger to you."

Vijaya, the companion of the Goddess, was enraged to hear these words of the messenger and drove her away. The latter, thoroughly upset returned to Mahisha who thereupon came along with many *asuras* to seize the Goddess. The march of his army of elephants, chariots, cavalry and infantry filled the earth and his banners atop the chariots fluttered high up in the sky while martial music rent the air. His commanders were all *asuras* named Karala, Dhurta, Vichashnu, Vikaralaka, Bhaikkala, Durmukha, Chanda, Prachanda, Amarasura, Mahahanu, Mahdmauli, Ugrasya, Vikatekshana, Jvalasya and Dahana and they were leading the fierce army of the demon.

The Goddess heard the clamour and realized that Her worship was being interrupted. She therefore ordered

Durga, one of Her innumerable manifestations, to destroy the approaching *asura* and his army. The latter mounted Her lion and with weapons in Her hands roamed about at the foot of Aruna Hill. She looked like the goddess Kalika. Roaring terribly and displaying its cruel teeth the lion advanced briskly. Durga produced from Her body the *Yogini Chakra* containing thousands of *matriganas* (women warriors) to slaughter the *asura* army. Durga's army looked more formidable and fearsome than that of Mahisha.

Then there commenced a fierce and awesome battle between the hosts of *yoginis* and the *asuras*. That part of the earth was covered with the slaughtered bodies of the *asuras*. The army of Mahisha was completely annihilated. It was a veritable feast for the hungry harpies and vultures. The celestial beings hailed this victorious event by showering flower petals on the army of Durga. Now, only the commanders and Mahisha himself were left on the battlefield. The various manifestations of Durga, namely, Brahmi, Varahi, Vaishnavi, Kaumari, etc, fought with the *asura* commanders and killed them.

Finally, Mahishasura himself alongwith his demons came to the battlefield. Unable to face him, the army of Durga prayed thus, "Taking the form of *yogic* sleep jestingly you closed the lotus eyes of Vishnu. Once you confronted Madhu, Kaitabha and, as desired by them, killed them through the power of Vishnu. But for you who took the form of Kausiki and killed Sumbha and Nisumbha, the protectors of the cardinal points could not have obtained their wealth. As a reward for the austerities performed by the King of Vindhya you began to dwell on the Vindhya mountains where even huntresses obtained your grace. Once you took away the very life force (*prana-sakti*) of *daityas* as requested by Kubera. You are Brahma's power of creation, Vishnu's power of sustenance and Rudra's power of destruction. Taking birth as a daughter of Yasoda and Nanda, you helped Krishna in killing Kamsa. You are called variously as Vidya, Maya, Lakshmi, Saraswati, Devi, Parvati and Durga."

On hearing these praises of the *matriganas*, Durga promised to protect them. With great power She went in person to face Mahishasura. She killed Prachanda with the scimitar (*mandalagra*), Chamara with the weapon *Pindipala*, Mahamouli with Her long sword, Mahahanu with the weapon known as *Karpara*, Ugravakta with the axe, Vikataksha with the weapon *Sakti*, Jwalamukha with the hammer and Dahana with the pestle. She then charged forth to attack Mahisha. He let out a hideous roar and angrily shot arrows aimed at Her. Durga too shot arrows at him, at his charioteer, at his chariot, at his flagpole and at those who were helping him in the chariot. Mahisha immediately attacked Her with the fierce weapon *Sataghni* (that which kills hundreds of persons). *Devas* and *matris* cried in fear. But the Goddess seized that weapon without any effort. He then attacked Her with many strange and powerful weapons. But none of them injured Her. The Goddess seized with Her hands all the missiles that were sent towards Her and broke them as easily as an elephant breaks a sugarcane. Devi's mount, the lion, also lashed at the *asura* with its tail, bit him with its teeth, mauled him with its nails and thus harassed him. He then rapidly assumed, one after another, the forms of a lion, a boar, a tiger, an elephant and a byson and fought with Durga. In the form of the byson he repeatedly butted at Devi and the lion with his horns. At one moment he was seen standing on the earth, the next he flew in all directions in space and immediately afterwards disappeared from sight.

Durga then severed his head with Her trident. Her army praised Her valour. As he fell with a terrible roar the Goddess took his head in Her hand and danced. When Mahishasura, the enemy of the world, was slain by Durga in this manner the *devas* danced with joy, the *Maharshis* rejoiced and the heavens showered flowers.

# XI. Parvati Praises the Lord of Arunachala

MARKANDEYA asked Nandikesvara: After killing Mahishasura, in what manner did the daughter of the king of the mountains practise austerities?

Nandisa said: Durga held the *asura's* head in one hand, and with the other which held the sword, did Her obeisance to Goddess Gowri. The latter looked with great kindness at Durga and said, "Dweller on the Vindhyas! You have achieved a formidable task. My austerities will now be completed without any obstacle. Your actions purify the world. Therefore please throw away the terrible head of Mahisha." On hearing this Durga tried to throw it away but could not shake it off Her hand. She was distressed.

Gautama then spoke to Durga, "Please create a new and sacred *tirtha* and bathe in it, then your sin will he expiated." Durga cleft a rock with Her sword. Immediately clear water gushed out of the rock. Calling out Arunachala's name '*Namah Sonadrinathaya*' (Prostrations to the Lord of the Red Hill), Durga bathed in that *tirtha*. Then the *linga* which had stuck in Mahisha's throat fell and was installed by Durga as Papanasana. Thereafter the *asura's* head slipped from Her hand. She then made Her obeisance to the Lord of Papanasana and circumambulated him. Gautama praised Her. When next She stood before Sri Gowri the latter realised that She was absolved of the sin of killing Mahisha. Turning to Gautama She said, "Although Mahishasura was wicked he had a *Sivalinga* inside his throat. It was I that ordered Durga to kill him. Therefore you must prescribe something for the expiation of my sin too."

Upon this Gautama said, "Goddess! By merely thinking of you, who are the power which creates, sustains and destroys the worlds, all the worlds become pure. If you still ask me to prescribe, it can only be to uphold *dharma*. If one transgresses *dharma* the others too will do so. I shall prescribe a *karma* (religious observance) which will expiate your sin. If, on completion of your penance and worship, on the full moon day in the month of *Kartika* you have *darshan* of this Hill your sin will be expiated and all your desires will be fulfilled."

When Gowri heard these words She immediately began to practise severe austerities. Surrounded by the flames of the five fires, She meditated on Her Lord. The auspicious full moon day of *Kartika* soon dawned. On the evening of that day a divine effulgence was seen on the peak of the Red Hill. She saw that it was blazing forth without any fuel or wick. She was wonderstruck at it and circumambulated the Hill, making obeisance to the Lord Iswara at every step and praised Him with love and devotion.

On seeing the Goddess who stood praising Him, the Lord appeared before Her and with great compassion, revealed to Her His universal form. He praised Parvati who had undergone severe penance and untold hardships in order to win His love.

Upon this Brahma, Saraswati, Vishnu, Lakshmi, Indra, the protectors of the cardinal points, *gandharvas*, *apsaras*, *vasus*, *devas*, sages, the eleven *Rudras*, the twelve *adityas*, hosts of *bhairavas*, *pisachas*, *vetalas* and *bhutas*, surrounded Mahesa and followed Him. The Goddess who saw Isvara approaching Her rejoiced greatly. She forgot the misery which She had endured on account of their separation. She was overcome with joy. Siva alighted from His mount, took Her hand and spoke to Her. "Goddess! You are fit to be adored by everyone. I too adore you. I am Narayana, you are Lakshmi; I am Brahma, you are Saraswati; I am Nagendra, you are Varuni; I am Chandra (moon), you are Rohini (his consort); I am Agni, you are Swaha! I am Surya (Sun), you are Suvarchala; I am the ocean, you are the Ganga; I am Meru, you are Urvara; I am Indra, you are Indrani; I am Kamadeva, you are Rati Devi; I am Ego, you are the *buddhi* (intellect); I am the wind, you are *sama* (stillness); I am the sea, you are the wave; I am *Purusha*, you are *Prakriti*; you are Knowledge, I am the object of Knowledge; you are the word, I am its meaning; I am Isvara, you are a part of me. It is by our command that the acts of creation, sustenance and destruction are carried on. You and I are inseparable. You separated yourself of your own accord and took on a form and underwent severe penance. I shall reward you for your love for me. Henceforth you shall be part of me and shall become the left half of my person."

Goddess Uma thus won the left portion of Siva and Arunachala thenceforth was hailed as *Ardanarisvara*. The Lord addressed Her, "Goddess! We shall remain inseparable. You shall be known as Apitakuchamba. Let the devotees at this sacred place worship you as Apitakuchamba and me as Arunachala and gain all pleasures and finally attain Liberation."

"As Durga, the slayer of Mahisha is a part of you, She shall abide here conferring the benefits of *mantras*, upon those who repeat them. This *Khadga Tirtha* will remove all the diseases and sins of those who bathe in it even once. Gautama who initiated you into austerities shall always be remembered. All my *ganas* and *devas* and gods shall dwell in this temple of mine. I shall ever abide here as Arunachala. And you as Aruna (feminine form of Arunachala). All *siddhis* will be attained here without difficulty."

Those who read these words of comfort spoken to Parvati, the daughter of the king of the mountains will be absolved of all sins and gain *svarga* and liberation.

# XII. The Benefits of Pradakshina and the Story of Vajrangada

MARKANDEYA said: Lord Nandikesvara! I have listened with great joy to your narration of the glory of Arunachala. Kindly narrate the story of Vajrangada, the Pandya King.

Nandikesvara replied:

Son of Mrikandu! It is on account of your steadfast devotion to the Lord of the *bhutas* (Siva) that you have become immortal (*chiranjivi*). Listen. In days of yore there lived a Pandya King named Vajrangada. He always followed the *dharma* and was just, dignified, skilful, patient, calm, humble and intelligent. He was a great devotee of Siva. After conquering his enemies he ruled over all the kingdoms from Kedara (in the Himalayas) to Setu (in the extreme south).

Once he set out hunting, riding a noble horse and entered a forest which extended as far as Arunachala.

Seeing a fine civet cat he desired to capture it and urged his horse towards it. The cat fled around the Sona Hill. When the horse followed it the king fell down overpowered by weariness like a person who is thrown out of *svarga* after enjoying the fruits of his good deeds. He said to himself, "How did I, for no reason at all, lose my strength? Where is the horse which carried me? It is not to be seen." Pondering thus he became confused and bewildered. At that moment there appeared a light in the sky like a flash of lightning. Even as he looked at it the cat and the horse left their bodies on the earth and rose into the sky in the form of celestial beings. The king stood looking at them in wonder. They showed their bright forms as if to remove the darkness of his confusion and addressed him, "O King, do not grieve over the loss of your horse and the civet cat. Know that we both have been thus transformed by the grace of the Sona Hill."

At this the king was relieved and asked them humbly with folded hands, "Who are you? How did this happen? Please tell me." Upon this one of the celestial beings turned to the king and said, "O King, we were in our previous lives *vidyadharas* known as Kaladhara and Kantisali. Once both of us went to the remote woods on the Meru Mountain where Durvasa was practising austerities.

"Kanthisali roamed about noisily hither and thither in a garden of flowers. I was attracted by the fragrance of the flowers and began to pluck them. At that moment, the extremely irritable sage Durvasa who was seated on a tiger skin under a *Shandiya* tree and glowing by virtue of his austerities like a blazing fire, looked at us with anger. We trembled. He said: 'Who are you who have brazenly trespassed into my hermitage and are destroying my garden? Even the sun and the moon dare not set foot in this sacred forest meant for my austerities. It is reserved for the worship of Siva alone. The wind shall not blow in it, nor shall bees enter it. Of the two who have defaced my garden, one shall be born as a horse and carry others. The other who was enamoured of the fragrance of flowers shall become a civet cat at the foot of a hill.' In this manner he cursed us.

"On hearing this curse we were thoroughly frightened and fell at his feet and begged, 'O Sage! Kindly forgive us for trespassing into your territory. We in our ignorance plucked the flowers. Save us.'

"On hearing our plea, Sage Durvasa, his anger now appeased, took pity upon us and mercifully said that the curse could be lifted only by circumambulating the Arunachala Hill. He further told us that once upon a time when Mahadeva was sitting in state with Indra, Upendra, the *dikpalakas* and others adoring him, a nymph named Nandana offered Him a fruit. Gajanana and Shanmuga, being boys, both desired to have it. But their father said, 'I shall give it to him who goes around the world and comes to me first'. Hearing this Skanda hastily started going round the world. Vinayaka, on the other hand, went round the Arunachala Hill and quickly came and stood before his father. The latter appreciated Vinayaka's intelligence and affectionately kissing him gave him the fruit. He also bestowed upon him the power to fulfil the desires of his devotees. Turning next to the *devas* and others in the assembly, Siva declared: He who circumambulates with devotion the Sona Hill which is verily my form, becomes like me (*saroopya*). He becomes the Lord of the entire world and reaches the highest state.

"Having fallen into the curse of the extremely irate sage and being tormented by the black (*kalakuta*) poison of his curse we took birth as a horse and a civet cat on earth."

Kaladhara continued:

"This Kantisali was born as a horse in Kambhoja and became your mount. I became a civet cat and roamed about the foot of this Hill. We were fortunate enough to circumambulate it as a result of your desire to hunt. You are a noble soul. But, as you circumambulated on a mount, you met with this misfortune. As we went on foot we regained our old state. O Indra among kings! Although we were born as animals we were liberated by your help. We shall now go back to our region. May Arunachala bless you." Thereupon, with folded hands, the king made his obeisance to Kaladhara and Kantisali who were about to return to their celestial region, and said: You have been released from your curse. What about my fate? When I think about it I feel distressed.

When he spoke thus Kaladhara and Kantisali said, "Listen carefully to what we have to say about your Liberation. Make the mind pure, control it and surrender it to Siva who is the cause of the creation, sustenance and destruction of the world. You have clearly realized from what happened to us that the Lord of the Arunachala Hill is a repository of compassion and that His glory is infinite. Circumambulate the Arunachala Hill on foot. Worship the Lord of Arunachala with flowers smeared with the fragrance of civet. Build quandrangles and towers at the temple of Arunachala according to your means. Your desire will be fulfilled. You will then become superior to Puru, Mandhara, Nabhaga, Bhagiratha and other sages."

After uttering these words they departed and Vajrangada became a staunch devotee of Lord Arunachala.

## Vajrangada Attains Salvation

Markandeya said:

Bhagavan! I have listened to your nectar-like story. I have also listened to the story of the *vidyadharas*. How long and in what manner did Vajrangada worship Siva? How did the Lord of Aruna bless him?

Nandisa replied: Vajrangada abandoned the idea of returning to his kingdom and erected a dwelling for himself near Gautama's *ashram* at the foot of the Aruna Hill. His army consisting of elephants, cavalry, chariots and infantry and his advisers, ministers, commander-in-chief, friends, relatives and servants came to see him. He received them with a steadfast mind, stopped them outside the city and surrendered his entire wealth to the Lord of the Sona Hill.

Along with his advisers, he engaged himself in the worship of Siva. He crowned his son Ratnangada king.

He worshipped the Lord of Sona with the numerous articles sent by the latter. He dug ponds around the hill, created gardens and gifted lands to *brahmins*. As the country around the Aruna Hill is an arid area, he dug hundreds of ponds and built numerous reservoirs. He invited his subjects who were with him to join him in his worship and service of the Lord of Sona.

He took delight in worshipping the Lord of the Aruna Hill in the company of Agastya who had arrived with his wife Lopamudra. Everyday after bathing in the tanks he performed *puja* to Arunachala. He went round the Hill on foot twice daily, repeating the Lord's name the while. He celebrated the *Karthikai Deepam* festival in a grand manner on the full moon day of the month of *Kartika*.

He anointed the *Linga* of Arunachala with fragrant water kept in golden pots and scented with fragrant flowers and camphor. He celebrated festivals every month in a befitting manner as laid down in the *agamas*. He laid the *giripradakshina* path (a distance of about eight miles) and made it fit even for *anga-pradakshina*. While going around the hill, with great devotion he would exclaim, "O Lord of the Aruna Hill, Ocean of Compassion! Lord of Apitakuchamba, my obeisance to Thee!" and become immersed in an ocean of bliss.

The Lord mounted on Nandi, accompanied by the Goddess Uma, *rishis* and *Sivaganas* hailing His glory appeared before the king. On seeing the God of Gods, Vajrangada fell at His feet with all the limbs touching the ground (*ashtanga vandanam*). Overcome with joy he folded his hands respectfully and said, "Lord of the *devas*! Kindly forgive the offences committed by me, an ignorant man weighed down by his *karma*." When he prayed very humbly in this manner the Lord of the Aruna Hill, the embodiment of the ocean of mercy, said:

"Child! Fear not! You are blessed. I assumed eight forms solely for the sake of all beings. In your previous life you were Purandara (Indra) living on the Kailasa mountain. Being arrogant you forgot me. In order to correct you, I made you undergo physical suffering which made you realise your folly and feel contrite. You prayed for liberation which is the source of true bliss. I bid you be born on earth as Vajrangada and obtain my grace. Therefore you were born in this place which is sacred to me. As you were ignorant you were instructed by the *vidyadharas* and others. You are now my great devotee. I am pleased with your worship and service. I shall now instruct you. Listen.

"This world of moving and stationary beings is made up of my eight forms, namely ether, air, fire, water, earth, sun, moon and *jivas*. I, as Time, bring together objects, *jivas* and way of action (*gati*). As for me, I transcend the fundamentals (*tattvas*); there is nothing beside me who am Siva.

"Brahma, Vishnu, Rudra, Indra and other *devas* are but waves which have arisen from me. Vani, Lakshmi, Ksharna, Sraddha, Prajna, Svahav, Svadha and others are but a shadow of my unlimited powers. Goddess Gowri, the Mother of the world, represents my divine illusion as *maya*. It is through Her that the universe appears and disappears. Creation, sustenance and destruction take place through Her. I display out of my freewill, this wonderful world which is like a picture. Your delusion has disappeared. You shall, by my grace, hereafter investigate the truth. You are not separate from me even as the waves are not different from the sea. Therefore you obtained a kingdom. You shall enjoy these luxuries as tokens of my grace. Afterwards you shall become Purandara again and enjoy celestial luxuries for a long time. Finally you shall unite with me." Saying this Siva disappeared. King Vajrangada continued to worship the Lord of Sona and finally merged in Him.

I have thus described to you the glory of Siva, the importance of devotion and the benefits of circumambulation of the Hill. What more is necessary? Circumambulation of the Sona Hill is more meritorious than a hundred horse-sacrifices. Further, the circumambulation of this Hill is more meritorious than all austerities. When it is made at auspicious times it will confer immeasurable benefit. There is no other place except Arunachala, no God except the Lord of the Aruna Hill.

On hearing Nandikesvara speak thus, the son of Mrikandu (*i.e.* Markandeya) shed tears of joy and became immersed in a sea of bliss.

## END OF PART II

# PART - III

This part deals with Glory of Arunachala as found in the centre portion of '*Siva Bhakta Mahatmyam*'. This is narrated by Sri Upamanyu Maharshi wherein, while describing the saint-poet Jnanasambandha's visit to Arunachala, the Glory of Arunachala is deleniated.

# I. Visit of Sambandha to Arunachala

UPAMANYU said: When Tirujnanasambandha (one of the four great Tamil saints) was staying at Tiruvarayaninallur (adjoining Tirukkoilur) adoring the Lord there, some of his followers pointed out Arunachala standing majestically at a distance. The child saint spontaneously composed a hymn of ten stanzas beginning with the words: '*Unnamulai Umayalodum*', meaning, the Lord who is accompanied by Uma known as Unnamulai.

Once he was looking for someone who would show him the way to Arunachala when he saw a strange looking old *brahmin* gathering flowers. He was moved by the sight of the old man and asked him respectfully, in a voice choked with emotion, "Where have you come from? Which is your place? Why have you come here?" The old man replied, "I have come from Arunachala. That is where

I live. I have come to gather flowers for the Lord." At this, Jnanasambandha asked him, "How far is Arunachala from here? Is it a small wood or a big forest? Kindly lead me for I do not know the way." The old man said, "Yonder is the Hill. It is not very far. I am old but I come here everyday and return with flowers required for the morning worship of the Lord. I shall take you there quickly by a good path". He then gathered some flowers and got ready to start.

Sambandha now asked him eagerly, "I wish to hear in detail about Arunachala." Thereupon the old man began to describe with great emotion, one after another, stories that spoke of the glory of Arunachala.

# II. The Manifestation of Arunachala and the Arrival of Parvati

THE old man said: Arunachala is a manifestation of the God wearing the crescent moon upon his head (*i.e.* Siva). It is a manifestation of Sambhu who in ancient times appeared as a column of fire in order to settle a dispute between Brahma and Vishnu. Brahma and Vishnu emerged from Sadasiva. Both became haughty and once argued as to who was the superior of the two. They fought fiercely. When the quarrel became severe and worldly activites were in danger of disruption, the Supreme Being Siva reflected thus, "If I do not appear before the quarrelling gods and make them realize their folly there will be an untimely dissolution of the universe." Resolving this He appeared between the quarrelling gods as a column of fire. They looked in wonder at that blazing column which extended from heaven to the nether regions. They became curious and attempted to find the summit and bottom of that column. Vishnu assumed the form of a boar and proceeded to discover its base by delving deep into the earth. Brahma took the form of a swan and soared to discover its top. Vishnu penetrated the earth as far as *rasatala* (one of nether worlds), but could not discover the origin of the column. Brahma too could not see the top even though he flew to the very edge of *Brahmanda* (*i.e.* the cosmos). Both of them, therefore, discontinued their efforts and returned to the earth with tired snout and wings and met each other. "What can this Column of Effulgence be whose top and bottom cannot be espied?", they exclaimed in wonder. Their ego-sense completely destroyed in the effort they became humble and pious.

At that instant a voice from the sky said, "This column is a manifestation of Sambhu. It has appeared with the object of blessing you. All moving and stationary beings and yourselves have come out of it. Until now neither of you knew Sambhu, the Omnipresent Being who transcends space and time, and each of you had, out of egoism and vanity vied with each other for superiority." When they heard the voice from the sky speaking thus, they addressed the Lord, "Obeisance to Sambhu who has assumed the form of a *linga*, and who exists in all moving and stationary beings, transcends everything, and who is the source of everything and has now taken the form of a column of dazzling effulgence. Great Lord! Kindly bestow Thy grace upon us. Reveal Thy true form to us, who are enveloped by the darkness of ignorance."

When the three-eyed Siva was praised thus by His sons He became gracious and appeared before them. He said, "I am pleased with you because your hearts are now full of devotion. I have come here to grant your prayers. Express your desires." On hearing these words, they said, "Lord of the worlds! We wish to have unfaltering devotion for Thy lotus feet. We should not become arrogant again. This is a column of grandeur and beauty bestowing grace on us. Thou shouldst always abide here in this form. Kindly withdraw Thy blazing Effulgence and abide as a *Linga* with the name of Arunachala for the welfare of the world. Otherwise the worlds will get scorched by Thy Effulgence. Let those who worship this *Linga* attain prosperity and Liberation". As Brahma and Vishnu prayed thus, the great God, the abode of compassion, said, "Let it be so."

Although the Lord is Being-Consciousness-Bliss (*Satchidananda*), He continued to abide in the form desired by Brahma and Vishnu.

The old man said, "Friend! Listen to this also. Parvati practised austerities here and won the left half of Arunachala." Upon this Sambandha requested the old man to narrate the story of Parvati's *tapas*, and Her ultimate reunion with Lord Siva.

## Parvati's Penance and Her Arrival at Arunachala

The old man replied: The great God once went with Parvati into a spacious hall revered by all the *devas*. It contained heaps of jewels and was supported by thousands of bejewelled columns. It was situated on the top of the Kailasa mountain amidst groves of wish-fulfilling trees. There the guileless Parvati, who thought that Her Lord was completely under Her influence, came behind Him silently and gently and playfully covered with Her lotus-hands the three eyes of Sambhu, the *Sadguru* of all the worlds, thinking, 'Let me see what He will say if I close His eyes'.

As soon as She closed those eyes which were actually the sun, the moon and Fire of Knowledge (*jnana*), darkness enveloped the universe for a long time. Although She covered the eyes for a few moments, it was millions of years for the universe. The darkness brought on by the playful act of the Goddess led to the gradual dissolution of the universe. The perturbed *devas* thereupon prayed to Siva to remove the darkness. Siva then ordered Gowri to take off Her hands. Goddess Uma immediately withdrew Her hands. At once, the entire cosmos came out of darkness. Sambhu chided Uma for Her thoughtless act, an act which led to the dissolution of the world. It was unbecoming of Her, the Mother of the universe. Only the Lord withdraws the worlds into Him at the time of *Mahapralaya*. But She out of Her ignorance had brought about an untimely *pralaya*. When Parvati, the beloved of Sambhu, heard the chastisement of Her Lord, She was upset. She realised that She had transgressed *dharma* and in a tone of repentance asked Her Lord what She should do to expiate this act of hers. Sambhu said, "What expiation shall I prescribe for you who are my very Self? Nevertheless I shall prescribe an atonement in accordance with the custom of the world. There is a famous, prosperous and sacred city on earth named Kanchi. There is a holy river (*tirtha*) named Kampa there which cleanses the sins of the people who take a dip in it. You may if you wish, undergo penance there and then rejoin me." On hearing these words Parvati proceeded to Kanchi.

The old man continued:

The Goddess Parvati practised austerities on the bank of the river Kampa, observing punctiliously and simultaneously the thirty-two kinds of *dharma*. She made a *linga* of sand and worshipped it with reverence. Wishing to test Her devotion Siva made the river rise in flood. Fearing that the *linga* of sand would be washed away, She embraced it and did not stir from the spot. Later, Manmatha (the god of love) installed it as Ekambaresvara, which bore the imprint of Her breasts and bangles. Then Siva's voice was heard from the sky. "Let this *linga* which has been worshipped by you remain here for the welfare of the world. I myself abide on earth as an effulgent hill known as Arunachala which grants the prayers of devotees. You may go there and with the guidance of Sage Gautama, continue to practise your austerities near his *ashram*. Afterwards I shall reveal to you my form of effulgence." On hearing these words the Goddess proceeded to Gautama's *ashram*. the Sage welcomed Her with due honours. He said, "I know that you have come here at Siva's bidding. I realise that He wants to protect His devotees at this place.

"Of all the abodes of Siva this is the most important. The God of gods manifested here for the sake of Brahma and Vishnu. At their request he assumed the form of a Hill known as Arunachala. It now shines with subdued Effulgence. After ninety-six Brahmas had come into existence and merged again in Sadasiva a new Brahma emerged out of Vishnu's navel and created the universe. He once created, at Indra's request, a woman of extreme beauty who was capable of attracting even the attention of *yogis*. But on seeing her enchanting beauty Brahma himself became enamoured of her and tried to capture her. She ran hither and thither to escape from him. When he tried to possess her forcibly she ran away in the form of a doe. Brahma then assumed the form of a stag and pursued her. She became a dove and flew away. Brahma flew after her in the form of a male bird. When she was pursued in this manner she sought refuge in Arunachala and cried out in agony. 'O refuge of the distressed, protect me!' Immediately a hunter came out of the *Linga* of Arunachala, bow in hand, to fight with Brahma who became free from his passion and regained his equilibrium. Turning to Arunachala he prayed, 'Thou must kindly pardon my misdeed'. At this the merciful Siva rose out of the *Linga* and said to Brahma: O Brahma! All the sins committed by you were expiated the moment you set eyes on Arunachala. There is no doubt about this. You can only realise a part of myself at Kailasa, Meru, Mandara and other sacred mountains, but in Arunachala you can realise my entire Self. O creator of the universe! You shall, after taking bath in the *Brahma tirtha* and adoring me, circumambulate me and be absolved of your sin. On hearing these words Brahma bathed in the *tirtha* in the prescribed manner and circumambulated Arunachala with his mind absorbed in Siva. As a result of this he again became the ruler of the world of the *devas*."

# III. Gautama Describes the Glory of Aruna Hill

GAUTAMA continued: Once Narayana continued to sleep even after a *kalpa* (a cycle of four *yugas* or aeons) had ended and hence the world was enveloped in darkness. The immortal *devas* were in distress. They thought of Mahadeva, the controller of everything and prayed to Him to save His creation. Siva thereupon created the *devas* who were thirty-three crores in number. They awakened Narayana from whose navel a lotus sprang up. As soon as he woke up he said to himself, "I slept when I should not have done so. I was under the influence of Siva's *maya*. What shall I do to expiate the sin of sleeping at an untimely hour? I shall seek refuge in Siva and expiate all my sins." At that moment he saw before him, Siva as pure Effulgence. He bowed to him respectfully and pleased Him with his adoration. Looking at Narayana who stood there praising Him with folded hands, Siva said, "I abide on earth in the form of Arunachala Hill. The moment you see me in that form you will cease to be ignorant. One of the Vishnus who were your predecessors obtained a boon from me at Arunachala. As the interior of the Hill is filled with fire, the rains falling on it from the clouds fear to run down it as streams. They are quite unable to leave it. That is why all one's sins are expiated by merely looking at it. All the wishes of devotees are fulfilled there. You shall again become the protector of the world by bowing down to that Hill and worshipping it." Having issued this command Siva disappeared.

Vishnu was relieved when he heard these words. He came to Arunachala, bathed in the Brahma *tirtha* and worshipped Arunachala Hill with a tranquil mind. Thereby his sins were expiated and again regained his position as protector of the world. It is by worshipping it that Surya (the sun god) became the ruler of all the planets. When Daksha Prajapati worshipped it, his curse was lifted and he became prosperous. Indra who had slain the *asura* named Vritra got over his afflictions and became King of the *devas* again and worshipped Arunachala. Similarly *siddhas, charanas, gandharvas, devas, vidyadharas* and others had their wishes fulfilled by worshipping Arunachala Hill. The Sun god abides on its eastern side, Visvamitra on the southern side, Varuna on the western side and Trisula on the northern side. These four *devatas* (deities) worship the Red Hill from four hills which form its boundaries at a distance of three *yojanas*. On its northern slope there stands a banyan tree which throws shade all around. The great Isvara (Siva) abides under it in the form of a *Siddha Purusha*. There are eight *lingas* at the eight cardinal points round the Hill. There is also a temple near it, built by the *devas* for the devotees of Siva. Inside that temple there is a *bakula* tree under which Siva is worshipped by Vamadeva. Agastya and Vasishtha each installed a *linga* there. They worshipped Arunachala and gained extraordinary benefit from their austerities. The holy river Sona flows near it as a clear stream. The sacred river Pennai also flows round it. I (Gautama) too adore Siva by practising austerities here and worship the ethereal *Linga* of Arunachala for the welfare of the world. In olden days kings overcame their enemies, regained their kingdoms and enjoyed prosperity and sovereignty by worshipping the Lord of Sonadri. O Goddess! If you worship this *Sivalinga* which is in the form of a Hill your austerities will fructify.

Sage Gautama also described to the Goddess as to how the fiery *Linga* cooled down:

This was a fiery Hill in the *krita yuga*, a ruby Hill in the *treta yuga*, a Hill of gold in the *dwapara yuga* and a rocky Hill in *kali yuga*. In the *krita yuga* the *devas* praised this fiery Hill from a distance, being unable to approach it. The Vedas refer to this Hill when they describe it as being copper-coloured, red and golden and the embodiment of all divine qualities. All the *devas* praised it and prayed, "Oh Supreme Self in the form of Aruna, the embodiment of all divine qualities! Obeisance to Thee! Pray, kindly cool down so that all can approach Thee!"

Upon this, the Hill ceased to be fiery and cooled down for the sake of devotees. There are many *tirthas* around it. Vishnu became sinless by bathing in the *Indra tirtha* situated to the east of it. By bathing in the *Agni tirtha* situated on its south-eastern side Agni was expiated of his sin of adultery. Yama became free of the sin of *brahmahatya* by bathing in the famous *Yama tirtha* to the south of the Hill. A travelling ascetic bathed in the *Nirriti tirtha* on its south-western side and thereby escaped from *bhutas* and *vetalas* (evil spirits). Varuna became the king of the oceans by bathing in the *Varuna tirtha* on the west. Vayu became the life-breath of the world by bathing in the *Vayu tirtha* on the north-west. Mahavishnu became the Lord of Lakshmi by bathing in the *Sona tirtha*, full of golden lotuses, on the north. The nine *grahas* (planets) attained that state consequent to their bathing in the *Isanya tirtha* on the north-east. The exceedingly glorious *Brahma tirtha* is in front of Arunachala inside His temple. It is guarded by Saraswati, Bhairavi, Ganapati, Durga and Skanda. In front of the Lord is situated the glorious *Siva tirtha*. It was in *Siva tirtha* that Bhairava got rid of Brahma's skull. Besides these, there are hundreds of *tirthas*, like the Ganga, the Vasishta, the Agastya, the Skanda, the Visvedeva and the Aswini. The Ganga worships the Sona Hill from the East, the Yamuna from the sky and the Saraswati from the head (*i.e.* top). All the sacred *tirthas* appear here to devotees at the time of worship.

When I prayed to the Lord as to how I should worship Him, the Lord of the Arunachala Hill graciously replied,

"I shall abide on earth in the form of an ethereal *Linga* in the sanctum sanctorum of the temple. You must worship this *Linga* according to the *agama sastras*. I, the Lord of the Arunachala Hill, the ethereal *linga* of fifty different colours, shall be worshipped through strength derived by austerities." After issuing this command, the great God, the Self-created Being, revealed Himself in the form of an extremely pure and ethereal *Linga*. When I saw it I felt that my goal had been attained and was blissful.

The Lord Himself prescribed the method of worshipping Him. At His command Visvakarma founded a prosperous city. Those who offer to the God of gods the ingredients necessary for His worship, enjoy luxuries in this world and attain, when they die, union with Arunachala. This *Linga* of Sambhu, which is made up of the eight constituents is full of effulgence. If one bows down to it and circumambulates it, one's sins will be burnt up. Those who circumambulate it are not reborn. They become eternal and merge into Arunachala.

One should, before proceeding to circumambulate the hill, take a bath, put on clean clothes, smear the body with sacred ash and put on a garland of *rudraksha* beads. One should walk slowly with a serene mind remembering Siva all the time. The very earth becomes taintless when the dust from the feet of those who walk on it, in circumambulation, falls on it. If one circumambulates the Hill by rolling on the ground all the way his body will at once become bright and hard like diamond. He will not pray for material happiness. Sambhu too circumambulates

Himself (*i.e.*, the Hill) during the six holy months of the sun's northern course (*Uttarayana*) in the company of *devas* and *rishis*.

One should never circumambulate the Hill on a conveyance. Once upon a time a King named Dharmaketu, who was well-versed in the rules prescribed for worshipping Siva, but indifferent to *dharma*, circumambulated the Hill on horseback. His horse became an object of adoration for the *devas* and was transformed into a *gananatha,* a leader of Siva's followers. It left the King and gained the abode of Siva. When the King saw his horse transformed into a leader of Siva's followers he also circumambulated the Hill on foot and became likewise a leader of Siva's followers. King Vajrangada lost his prowess as a result of violating the convention of the worship of Siva. He was however later reunited with Siva by virtue of his great devotion to the Lord. By circumambulating this Hill two *vidyadharas,* Kantisali and Kaladhara were absolved of the curse of Durvasa. They had been transformed into a horse and a civet cat, but by circumambulating the Hill they regained their state of *vidyadharas*.

In former times there was a Pandya King named Vajrangada. He made the earth tremble with the might of his arms. Once he went hunting in the forest adjoining Arunachala. Seeing a civet cat which exuded fragrance, he urged his horse towards it with the idea of capturing it. Chased by him it ran in great fear round the Sona Hill. Although the King was very strong, he fell down headlong from the horse breathing heavily, like a *jiva* falling from *svarga* on the expiry of its merit. While he lay in great distress, too weak even to get up, he saw before him two bright beings dazzling like lightning. Even as he looked at them he saw his horse and the civet cat cast off their bodies and assume divine forms. They narrated their story to the astonished king, "Oh King! We were originally leaders of *vidyadharas*. Once we were wandering about a wood near Durvasa's *ashram* close to Mount Meru. We were joyfully plucking the flowers in his garden. When he noticed us he said angrily, 'You in your arrogance have enraged me by treading on this holy ground. One of you shall be born on earth as a horse and become the mount of a king who will ill-treat him. The other who was enamoured of the fragrance of flowers shall become a civet cat in a dense forest on the slope of a hill.'

"When he cursed us in anger we prayed to him to forgive us. That great soul then bestowed his grace on us. He said, 'You will be released from your curse if you circumambulate the Arunachala Hill. The circumambulation of it is as good as circumambulating all the worlds. That is why Sankara gave the fruit to Ganapati who had first circumambulated the Arunachala Hill and not to Guha who had circumambulated all the worlds.' We were then transformed into a horse and a civet cat. As we circumambulated the hill on foot we have regained our original forms of *vidyadharas*. But, as you circumambulated on your horse, you met with this fate. You may also now circumambulate the Hill on foot. Worship the Lord with red lilies scented with civet. Erect towers and quadrangles in the temple of the universal Lord according to your might. You will soon become Devendra again." After saying this Kantisali and Kaladhara went away. Vajrangada then entrusted his kingdom to his son Ratnangada and made the city of Arunachala his permanent abode. He circumambulated the Sona Hill and attained *mahasiddhi*.

In former times, when in the form of a deer, Tilottama who was afraid of Brahma took shelter at Arunachala and begged the Lord to save her, the latter manifested as a hunter. At that very spot on the path of circumambulation he still abides in the same form. That is where Brahma and Vishnu worship Him. At the same place there are several *devatas* and *tirthas*. One can attain liberation there through gifts, austerities, sacrifices and worship.

Those who live at Arunachala with the object of serving the Lord are worthy of liberation. There is no sacred place comparable to Sona Hill, no *mantra* comparable to the *Panchakshara*, no devotee of Siva comparable to Vishnu and no talisman comparable to the sacred ash. Neither Kailasa nor the Mandara mountain can be a match to the Arunachala Hill on earth, for while they are the abodes of Siva, this Hill is Siva Himself.

The following incidents show that one can attain the goal of one's life by performing any act of devotion according to one's ability. A spider which happened to weave a web in a corner of the Aruna Hill became a king. That king remembered his past life and adorned the Lord of the Arunachala Hill with many clothes. While a thirsty elephant was drinking water it happened to spray some water on the Hill with its trunk and scatter wild flowers. As a result of this, it became a leader of the *ganas* and attained liberation. Even insects crawling on its slopes get rid of their sins and attain the world of Siva. A firefly happened to give light to a person who, carrying a load, came to rest at night on the slope of the Hill. As a result of this it attained liberation even while alive. A vulture flying in search of prey happened to remove the dust in front of Siva by flapping its wings. Immediately it attained supreme liberation. It is impossible therefore to describe the glory of the Lord of Arunachala, He of such wonderful powers that transcend thought and word.

Goddess! You may also adore the Lord of the Sona Hill whose attributes are infinite and get your desires fulfilled. Austere one! You will attain the object of your wishes and reunite with Sambhu. Austerities have been prescribed for you solely for the welfare of the world.

When Gowri heard the wise words of the sage She was filled with great joy. She praised him and told him, "I shall adore Siva at this very place and by pleasing him I shall be united with him."

Eager to begin Her austerities She asked him for a suitable hermitage. The sage assured Her that it would be provided.

# IV. The Slaying of Mahisha and the Form of Ardhanareeswara

UPAMANYU continued the narration: The old man said: At Sambhu's behest, the Goddess installed an image of Siva on the *Pavalakundru,* a spur of the Arunachala mountain. Then Goddess Parvati, with matted tresses, wore the bark of a tree. She smeared Her body with sacred ash and practised austerities as prescribed. She appointed Satyavati, Vanavaini, Subhaga and Bandhumari to guard Her *ashram* on all the four sides. She appointed Durga to carry out Her instructions and to guard the forest.

The *devas* who were afraid of Mahishasura (demon in the shape of a he-buffalo) prayed to Parvati and She assured them of Her protection, saying, "I shall kill him by a stratagem", and continued to practise Her austerities. Mahishasura, the enemy of the *devas,* who had become arrogant on account of a boon obtained by him, came hunting in the company of demons. While wandering about the forest he came accidentally to the wood in which the Goddess was performing *tapas*. When he tried to enter it, he was prevented by the guards and he stood still for a moment. Being a warrior with no scruples, he stopped his followers on the bank of the river in a dense forest and issued instructions to the demons who were adepts in producing illusions. Disguising themselves as ascetics they entered the woods and after seeing the Goddess returned to him and described Her beauty.

On hearing their words, that demon warrior became enamoured of Her and immediately ordered the *asuras* armed with numerous weapons to attack the guards at the hermitage. The four *Sakti Devis* retaliated with their dazzling and powerful weapons and slew all of them. Thereupon the enraged Mahishasura commanded four of his renowned generals to fight the *Devis*. When they also were killed in the fight with the *Sakti Devis*, he despatched more warriors until the fight escalated into a battle.

Parvati in the form of Durga then rose and entered the battlefield. With weapons blazing like flames in Her sixteen hands, She attacked Mahisha who came charging at Her fiercely. When Mahisha appeared on the battlefield with sword and shield, Durga armed Herself with a sword, shield and a discus. While the battle between Durga and Mahisha was raging, the *devas* prayed to Durga thus, "Devi! The world is suffering on account of the battle. It is but a sport to you. Mother of the world! Kindly end this game quickly for the welfare of the world."

Thus beseeched by the *devas*, the Goddess Durga threw Mahisha down and trod on him and pierced him with Her trident. Being caught thus the demon let out a scream. Durga severed Mahisha's head with Her sharp sword and danced upon it. The *devas* showered flowers upon Her and praised Her. The loud sound of the celestial musical instruments heralded the death of the cruel *rakshasa* and the arrival of peace.

The *devas* then appealed to Her, "Let that head be severed completely. It still appears to possess some life. Let us remember this form of Thine treading upon the body of the demon; also grant the boon that those who meditate on this form shall overcome all obstacles and finally attain liberation." The Goddess was pleased to say, "Be it so."

Parvati regained Her original form with matted locks wearing the bark of a tree as a garment and looked at the demon's throat which had been pierced. Seeing a *linga* inside, She held it in Her hands. The Goddess was unable to free Her hand of the *linga* as it stuck to Her palm. She exclaimed: Alas! What have I done! It is a devotee of Siva I have slain! She went to the Sage Gautama along with Her companions and said to him: I offered my protection to the *devas* who took shelter under me. In doing so I have in my ignorance slain Mahishasura, a devotee of Siva. The *Sivalinga* which was in his throat does not leave my hand. How shall I expiate the sin of having killed a devotee of Siva?

On hearing this, Gautama said: O Gowri! Do not fear. This *rakshasa* is not a devotee. He was a *siddha* in his past life. He became a bison on account of a curse; he was not only a demon, he used to eat human beings. The *Sivalinga* worn by one of the devotees of Siva who was unfortunate enough to be devoured by him got stuck in his throat. As he had a *linga* inside him when he died and as he came into contact with your divine lotus-like feet, his curse has been lifted. Whoever wears a *Sivalinga* certainly attains Liberation whether he does so with or without devotion and faith. Moreover, even heinous crimes for which no expiation has been prescribed, will certainly be forgiven when one has *darshan* of the Arunachala Hill. Notwithstanding the noble Gautama's assurance, the Goddess continued to feel penitence for Her act of slaying a devotee of Siva.

At this moment She heard a voice in the sky that addressed Her, "Cleave the earth with your sword. Out of that cleft will arise simultaneously the nine rivers, *viz.*, the Ganga, the Yamuna, the Sindhu, the Godavari, the Saraswati, the Sona, the Kaveri and the Narmada, all together. Bathe daily in this *Kadga tirtha* (the spring caused by the sword) for a whole month beginning on the day on which the moon is in the constellation *Jyeshta*, repeating the *aghamarshana mantra* (a *mantra* recited before taking a ritualistic bath). If you live near that *tirtha* no fear will be felt, there will be no drought and I shall be pleased. Leave the *linga* that is in your hand beside the spring, take a bath in it and worship the *linga* with due offerings. You must with a tranquil mind install that *linga* on the bank of the *tirtha* and name it Papanasa. You should perform a sacrifice, a *devayaga*, commencing on the asterism of *Uttarashada* and take the bath signifying its end on the asterism of *Krittika*. You should then in the manner prescribed worship me in the form of Arunachala. I shall then reveal to you my effulgent form."

Accordingly, Gowri cleft the earth with Her sword, and the nine *tirthas* came out in the form of a single spring. The Goddess to whose hand the *linga* continued to stick, bathed in it. The spring at once became blue on account of Her lustre. Her mind, which was agitated owing to Her separation from Her dear Lord became calm. She lived near that spring. After a month, She conducted a festival for the *devas,* a *devotsavam,* in the month of *Kartika* and worshipped Siva. On the day of *Krittika* in the evening She meditated upon the form of Siva: Lord of the *devas*! If I am fit enough to see your true form, pray, kindly reveal Thy form. At once the Effulgence of Siva in the form of the Arunachala Hill filled the entire world with its brilliance. And there arose from the Column of Effulgence a tawny complexioned and blue-throated Siva who said: Parvati! I am pleased with your penance and devotion. The sin, if at all it can be termed so, which you incurred by closing my eyes and plunging the universe in darkness, has now been expiated by having darshan of Arunachala. Uma! For your youthfulness you shall be known as Apitakuchamba. O Devi! Come to me and merge in me on completion of your circumambulation of Arunachala.

The Goddess then circumambulated this Hill as advised. Like a bride circumambulating the sacred fire at the time of Her marriage, the daughter of the mountain circumambulated Arunachalesvara in the company of Saraswati, Lakshmi, Indrani, Arundhati and the wives of sages. She prayed for union with Siva. After completing the circumambulation She prostrated before the Lord, stood with folded hands and earnestly prayed to Him. The Supreme Lord was thereupon pleased to appear before Her. The Goddess was overwhelmed with joy and ecstasy. She prostrated before Him and with folded hands prayed, "We two should never be separated. Thou must always abide here for the welfare of the world so that *devas*, human beings and others who adore Thee may have Thy *darshan* at all times." The Lord of Arunagiri acceded to Her prayer for the welfare of the world. He also gave Her one half of His body. He ordered Visvakarma — the celestial builder to build a city which the latter did. The city was named after the Hill as Arunachala. It is the first and most sacred of all ancient cities. Siva is still being worshipped there in the form of a Self-originated *Linga*. One becomes free of all sins the moment one remembers and adores Arunachalesvara, the Lord of Unnamulai. It is certain that those who read or hear or meditate upon this glorious story of Arunachalesvara will attain the immortal abode of Siva.

# V. Arrival of Sambandha at Arunachala

AFTER listening with great pleasure to the enchanting story of Arunachala as narrated by the venerable old man, Sambandha followed him along with his retinue. When they reached the precincts of Arunachala the old man leading them suddenly disappeared. He was none other than Arunachala who was leading his child to His abode.

In accordance with the Lord's command, His *bhutaganas* appeared as hunters and robbed the personal possessions of Jnanasambandha and his followers. They took away the bundles and ran away from the place.

The Saint thought: Alas! I cannot find the old *brahmin* who was leading the way, our only recourse now is to pray to the Lord who grants wealth and joy. When he sang the praises of the Lord, the extremely compassionate

Arunachala appeared mounted on Nandi along with His consort. When Sambandha saw the Lord, he with great devotion and overflowing love prostrated and with folded hands sang melodious hymns praising the Lord. The Lord with great affection and in a reverberating voice said: Child! Because of my love for you I wanted you to come to Arunachala which is my eternal abode. Hence I assumed the form of an old *brahmin* and came to the garden at Arayaninalloor in the guise of plucking flowers for the Lord's *pooja*. Upon my orders, *bhutaganas* took away your possessions. The belongings of your followers shall be returned. A feast shall be set before you and your followers so that your hunger may be appeased.

Sambandha and his followers got back whatever they had lost and a veritable feast was set before them. The Lord bade the child Saint to come to His temple. In ecstacy, Sambandha approached the Lord's temple whose mighty towers were visible from afar.

In every house the chanting of the Vedas could be heard. Great hospitality was shown to the guests by the residents of the holy city of Arunachala as if the former were the very form of Lord Siva. In the streets around the temple of Arunachala, the sounds accompanying the celebration of the festival for the deities could be heard. *Yagas* were being performed. The deities were brought out of the temple on procession accompanied by elephants, horses and chariots. Sambandha saw *tapasvis* who were deeply absorbed in the bliss of Siva. The city of Arunachala was a flourishing one with scholars well versed in the

Vedas and *sastras*, their bodies radiating the glow of intense *tapas*, devotees with Arunachala's name on their lips, wearing *rudraksha* and their frames smeared with *vibhuti, jnanis* who cared not for the state of Brahma or Indra and *yogis* who were immersed in their Heart in perfect bliss.

After passing the streets on either side of which stood many storied buildings, Sambandha reached the temple of the Lord. Sambandha entered the temple which had courts and majestic walls. With profound devotion and love for Arunachala he reached the *sanctum sanctorum* and surrendered himself. He circumambulated the Lord and the Goddess Apitakuchamba. He adored the Lord and paid his homage by praising Him with a decad beginning with the words '*Poovar malarkondu*'. He resided in the vicinity of Lord Arunachala for a few more days singing decads praising gloriously the Lord and the Hill of Arunachala. Sambandha and his followers left Arunachala after seeking the Lord's blessings and continued their journey.

## END OF PART III

# PART - IV

This is a commentary by Sri Vidhyeswara in *Siva Mahapuranam* dealing with the Glory of Arunachala

# EASY STEPS TO LIBERATION

SUTA said: O wise *brahmins*! As requested by Vyasa, Bhagavan Sanatkumara here gives the instructions regarding means to liberation.

There are three ways mentioned in the Vedas for attaining Liberation. These are, listening to the praise of Siva, singing His praise and meditating upon Siva.

The sages then asked Suta Muni: O Sage! You have prescribed the three ways viz., hearing the praise of Siva, singing His praise and meditating upon Him. But if one is unable to follow any of the above, tell us how, without much effort one can attain liberation.

Suta replied: If one is unable to study the scriptures and follow their dictat, he can install either Siva's idol or *linga* and engage in its worship everyday. In this way one can cross the ocean of *samsara*. Siva's grace alone is sufficient to attain Liberation. Many *rishis* of yore by merely worshipping *Sivalinga* or His idol have become *jivanmuktas*.

The *rishis* further asked: It is customary that all deities are worshipped in the form of idols. Kindly enlighten us as to why Siva alone is worshipped in both forms *i.e.* the idol as well as the *linga*.

To this Suta replied: O Sages! None but Siva can answer your question, for its significance is deep. However I shall tell you what Siva imparted through the line of *Sadgurus*. Siva alone exists as form and formless. He is the creator of the universe. In His transcendental form He assumed the form of *linga* and in His all pervading nature He assumed the form of an idol. Thus He is worshipped both as a *linga* and idol. He is the Supreme Being, the Absolute *Brahman*. The other deities do not possess *Brahmanhood* nor are they transcendental. They are thus worshipped only as idols with form and name. Sankara alone is *Brahman*. The others are only *jivas*. He is verily the *pranava,* the quintessence of all the Vedas.

In times of yore, on mount Mandaragiri, the same question was asked of Nandikesvara by Brahma's son, the wise Sanatkumara. Nandikesvara gave the same answer to Sanatkumara. Further Sanatkumara wanted to know about the manifestation of the *linga*. Nandikesvara answered thus: O child! I shall narrate to you what exactly happened in former times. There arose a quarrel between Brahma and Vishnu. In order to subdue their pride the Supreme Lord, the Absolute Brahman, manifested in the battlefield as a Column of Effulgence for the welfare of the world and revealed Himself as an Effulgent *Linga*. From thence the *Linga* became the symbol of *Brahman* transcending attributes and the idol became His form with attributes.

# 11. Quarrel Between Brahma and Vishnu

LONG ago while the glorious Vishnu was slumbering on Adisesha, along came Brahma quite unexpectedly and addressed Vishnu thus, "Who are you? Even on seeing me you are arrogant enough to continue reclining. Young one, get up. Look at me, your creator. Whoever insults the worshipful *Guru* is a traitor. Penance has been decreed for such a fool." Enraged by these words, but appearing calm and peaceful, Vishnu said, "Child! come, sit on this seat. Why does your face reflect an agitated mind?" Brahma replied, "O Vishnu, over the passage of time you have become proud. I am the protector of the world as well as of you." To this, Vishnu said, "Young one, this world is contained within me. You have risen as an offspring from the lotus of my navel. Your words are meaningless."

Nandikesvara said:

In this way both the conceited gods continued to tell each other, "I am the Lord, not you." They came to the point of destroying each other. Brahma took the form of a swan and Vishnu took the form of Garuda and began to battle like warriors. This fierce battle was witnessed by all the *devas*. The gods continued attacking each other with powerful weapons. The desperate *devas* said, "No one can lift even a blade of grass without the grace of the Supreme Being Siva who is the source of creation, protection and destruction." They went to Mount Kailas, worshipped Lord Ganesa and then had *darshan* of Mahesa who was enthroned with Uma and surrounded by the *sivaganas*. They prostrated to Siva who blessed them and uttered sweet and gracious words.

## The Manifestation of the Effulgent Linga

Mahadeva said, "Children, blessings on you. It was I who ordained the quarrel between Brahma and Vishnu in order to bring about the manifestation of the Effulgent *Linga*."

He then appeared on the battlefield. Seeing that Brahma and Vishnu were about to destroy the whole creation by the most powerful weapons, Lord Siva manifested before them as a glorious column of fire. Immediately, their weapons became powerless. Brahma and Vishnu wondered as to what this power was that could not be grasped by the senses. They decided to discover its source and end. Vishnu took the form of a boar and decided to search for the bottom of the column; while Brahma took the form of a swan and flew upwards in search of the summit. Hari could not get to the bottom of the column and he returned tired and weary. Brahma, while flying upwards saw a fragrant screw-pine steadily coming down. The flower informed Brahma that it had fallen from Siva's matted locks ages ago. It had been coming down ever since. It advised Brahma to give up the search for the summit. Brahma told the flower, "O friend, please bear witness before Vishnu that I saw the summit of the column." He also added that it was not against *dharma* to tell a lie in times of danger. Returning to Vishnu, Brahma produced the flower as witness and Vishnu was convinced. Vishnu thereupon prostrated before Brahma and worshipped him with all due honours. At that moment, Siva appeared from within the column of fire to punish Brahma for his deceit. They realised their folly in trying to measure the Infinite and begged for forgiveness. The Lord said, "Child Hari, though enamoured of power, you spoke the truth. Therefore, you shall be honoured by all mankind. Henceforth you shall have separate temples installed for your worship and festivals." He thus gave Vishnu a status equal to Himself.

# III. Arunachala Blesses Brahma and Vishnu

IN order to subdue the pride of Brahma, Mahadeva created a fearsome form called Bhairava and bade it teach Brahma a lesson. Bhairava cut off the fifth head of Brahma. Seeing this pathetic sight, Vishnu prayed to Siva, "O Lord, you yourself gave Brahma five heads as his characteristic feature. Therefore please forgive him and show him mercy." Siva was pleased and prevented Bhairava from proceeding further. Siva turned to Brahma and said, "Enamoured of power, you uttered falsehood. Henceforth there shall be no temple, nor worship offered to you in this world." Brahma said, "Lord, show mercy on me. I consider my beheading as a sign of grace. O Lord, one who tolerates the misdeeds of Thy children, kindly forgive my ignorance." The Lord said, "Because of your quarrel, the world is in darkness. Do undertake the burden of the world and sustain it. Although I have decreed that there may not be separate temples for you, I ordain that you shall be the presiding deity at *agnihotras* and other *yagnas.*" The Lord chided the screw-pine flower for its perjury and said that it would no longer decorate His matted locks and shall not be offered to Him in worship. Nevertheless, the merciful Lord declared that it would adorn His worshippers and His mount.

Further, Brahma and Vishnu performed *puja* to their beloved Lord. With great devotion they offered garlands, ornaments, bracelets, crown, sandal paste, fruits, frankincense, camphor, cloth made of pure silk, white umbrella, fan etc. The Lord was surrounded by His devotees and truly it resembled an emperor's majestic court. The merciful Lord gave away, with His infinite blessings, the articles offered to Him by the primal gods to His devotees present there.

The extremely pleased Lord Siva then graciously declared: This auspicious day on which the *devas* and gods worshipped me, shall be celebrated as *Sivaratri* throughout the world. He who worships me on that day shall attain noble qualities like fortitude etc., essential for an aspirant hankering after liberation. Morover worshipping me on that day will yield the total merit of adoring me with *pujas* etc., throughout the year. Just as tidal waves in the ocean are generated by the full-moon and new-moon, all *dharmas* shall bear fruit on *Sivaratri*.

In the month of *Marghasirsa* [December-January, when the sun is in the zodiacal sign of Sagittarius, when the moon is full, and the star *Aridra* (Plaedes) is in ascension], I manifested as a Column of Effulgence to subdue your pride. Hence on this day whosoever installs a *Sivalinga* or my idol and worships me, he shall be more dear to me than Subramanya.

This sacred place which served to kill your ego-sense shall be considered as the most powerful spiritual centre in the universe. I further decree that it shall yield all worldly pleasures. This Column of Effulgence which has no beginning or end shall become the nucleus of all forms and manners of worship. The very sight of this Hill, worshipping by touching it and meditating on it shall surely lead one to liberation. This shall become famous on earth as Arunachala. There shall be many sacred *tirthas*. Mere abidance and death in this place would ensure freedom for even insects and animals from the vicious cycle of birth and death. All virtuous deeds like feeding of the poor, offering alms to the needy, celebrating marriages of the poor, performing temple festivals, *yagnas* and chanting of my name will yield infinite merit. Of all shrines sacred to me this is the foremost one. By merely thinking of Arunachala one's ego is rooted out. This place shall excel all other places in spiritual aura, glory, mystical power, wealth and in granting the ultimate human goal. The one who worships me here, shall successively abide near me, attain my form and finally merge in me.

Nandikesvara continued: The Lord after blessing the now pious Brahma and Vishnu further addressed them:

Children! I alone am the 'formless-form'. I alone am Brahman. No other deity can be regarded thus and hence none else can be Isvara.

I alone exist as Effulgent *Linga*, as Idol and as Absolute Brahman. This has been described earlier. It is a wonder that in your ignorance forgetting me, who am the Supreme Being, you fought in vain. I alone shine as the Self in the inner core of every object in the universe. Every realised *jnani* declares thus. Because of my love for you I am repeating again and again the quintessence of all Vedas which reveal Brahman so that you might understand its import.

I am Brahman. All are my form. I am Isvara. I create, sustain, destroy, conceal, bless. All the five-fold *karmas* are mine alone. O Brahma and Vishnu! Being Perfect and Absolute I exist as Brahman. O Children! Being Omnipresent and dwelling in all, I am the Self of all. All those who are ignorant of this knowledge are *jivas*. In order to make you realise my Brahman-hood, I exist as Absolute form. Again in order to show you my Isvara-hood I emerged from the Effulgent Column as *Sivalinga*. Now you realise my state as both the Absolute form and the *Linga* form.

You may worship this Column of Effulgence as *Sivalinga*. This is verily my form. The worship of this alone is sufficient to attain my form. This glorious form of mine should be worshipped. I who transcend everything, shine as this *Linga*. One who installs this *Linga* and worships it will merge in me.

# The Five-Fold Divine Karma of Lord Arunachala

BRAHMA and Vishnu asked the Lord to graciously describe the aspects of His five-fold *karma*, to which Siva answered:

I shall now narrate my divine play which is not to be revealed. My five-fold karmas are to create, to sustain, to destroy, to conceal and to bless. The creation is the beginning of *samsara,* its continuation is sustenance, and its merging in me in dormant form is destruction, to confuse it is concealment and its final Liberation is due to my grace and blessing. If anyone declares that it is he who performs these *karmas,* he does not realise the truth. The five-fold *karmas* including that of liberating the *jivas* are my eternal divine play. The wise see all the five aspects in the five elements. That is, the earth forms the basis for creation, water sustains it, fire causes destruction, air conceals it and absolute space brings about liberation. This is realised by the *jnanis*.

I empowered you with two of my aspects *viz.*, that of creation and sustenance. And Rudra and Mahesvara were empowered to destroy and to conceal. I alone am entitled to bless my creation, show mercy and grace and finally liberate *jivas*.

Children! After acquiring form, name, mount and *karma*, weapon etc., through my grace you forgot to meditate upon me. Hence you fell into the ocean of ignorance. If you had been aware of my existence, then, like Mahesvara you would have remained without the ego-sense.

In order to get rid of your ego-sense meditate upon *pranava,* which is my first name. I shall initiate you now into that *Mahamantra* (the most sacred of all *japas*). This *pranava* originated from my face. It reveals my form that is verily my name. I am its meaning. Meditation upon the *pranava* is meditation on me. Every letter in *pranava* refers to my face. *Pranava* pervades all names and forms, Vedas and the *Upanishads*. This symbolises the unification of Siva and Shakti. From this emerged the *Panchakshara*. It is the source of all languages, the *Gayatri mantra*, the Vedas, and other *mantras*. While every *mantra* yields specific benefits, *pranava* alone can bestow all benefits on those who meditate on it. Further, after bestowing all earthly pleasures, this *mantra* alone leads to Liberation.

Nandikesvara said:

Isvara then initiated Brahma and Vishnu into the supreme *pranava japa* and blessed them. Brahma and

Vishnu offered themselves to the Lord as *gurudakshina*. They praised the Lord and made obeisance to Him. Isvara then advised them: Children! Meditate upon *pranava* into which I have initiated you. If you meditate on *pranava* when the star *Arudra* is in the ascent it shall bestow countless blessings on you. Aspirants desirous of liberation should meditate upon the *Sivalinga*. The installation of *Sivalinga* is an easy means to attain *mukti*. Having blessed both Brahma and Vishnu thus, the Lord ever abided in their hearts.

# The Greatness of Feeding at Arunachala

SANAKA requested Brahma to enlighten them about the benefits derived from conducting *annadana* (feeding of the poor) at Arunachala.

Brahma replied:

There is no good deed equal to *annadana* in the three worlds. *Annam* (rice) is the basis of *prana* (life-breath). Hence one who gives *annam* gives his *prana*. For this reason one who desires his own welfare should offer *annam* to the needy and the poor. If this is performed at Arunachala, he attains great merit and becomes the ruler of all the worlds. Neither Vishnu nor I can measure that merit. Even the giving of wealth and jewellery as charity cannot equal the merits obtained by *annadana* at Arunachala.

Once a king named Singadvajan, descendent of the famous *Surya vamsa*, ruler of the *Dravida* country, and known for his valour and generosity, was giving away jewels and diamonds to learned *brahmins*. In addition he gifted away everything that he possessed. He however did not perform *annadana* even once. When he died he was taken to the abode of *devas*. He was succeded by his son, Chitrakethu who excelled his father in might and valour. He too like his father gifted away land, jewels etc. But he too failed to perform *annadana*.

One day Singadvajan happened to meet the Sage Narada, the foremost of *rishis*, in the celestial region. Sage Narada said: O King! The feeding of the poor (*annadana*) supercedes all other gifts made on earth. It bestows knowledge of the Self, as the Supreme Lord dearly loves the one who performs *annadana*. You donated everything but you did not perform *annadana*. He who feeds the poor, is offered nectar in the heavens.

As requested by Singadvajan, Narada approached his son Chitrakethu on earth. Chitrakethu welcomed the Sage. After duly accepting his respects, Narada informed Chitrakethu that although his father Singadvajan gifted away everything he had not performed *annadana*. He alone who had fed the poor and the needy shall receive ambrosia in heaven. Hence Chitrakethu should perform *annadana* so that his father shall receive the ambrosia. The king decided to perform *annadana*.

However, the king wanted to know as to where on this earth *annadana* should be performed so that it shall bestow merits on him and his father. Narada informed him that the merit one obtained by feeding a lakh of people elsewhere cannot equal that of feeding one person in Kasi, and the merit gained by feeding just one poor *brahmin* at Arunachala will out-weigh that of feeding a crore at Kasi. Particularly if this was done on a *dwadasi* day (i.e. twelfth day counted from the day of new moon/full moon), it would be equal to the merit obtained by feeding the poor throughout the year.

After listening to the wise words of Sage Narada, Chitrakethu performed *annadana* everyday at Arunachala. By this act of the son, the father in the celestial region received nectar and in due course passed on to the various upper regions and finally merged in Siva. Hence everyone should endeavour to perform *annadana,* particularly at Arunachala, for it not only benefits the person who does it, but also bestows great spiritual merit upon his kith and kin.

## End of Part IV

# PART - V

# The Greatness of the Deepam Festival at Arunachala as Found in Skanda Purana

GODDESS Gowri requested Sage Gowthama to kindly expound to Her the greatness of the festival of light at Arunachala. Gowthama replied: Gowri! I shall describe to you the glory of that which liberates people from all sins and bestows all prosperity. In the month of *Karthika*, on the day of the star *Krittika* during *pradosha* (i.e. thirteenth day counting from the new moon/full moon) the fortunate ones who perform *giripradakshina* are not born again. All *karmas* are destroyed on performance of *giripradakshina*. It is customary to circumambulate the Hill for a *mandala* or forty days. One who is not able to do this may perform *giripradakshina* at least for eleven days. If even this is not possible, then one should go round the Hill on the day of the *Deepam*. This is equivalent to performing crores of *yagnas*. He who worships the *Deepam* lit atop the Hill derives countless blessings. A person residing elsewhere may light lamps in front of any shrine of Siva, atop His temple towers or on the peaks of other hills and he will be blessed. Whatever may be the attitude of the devotee, the mere lighting of the lamp on this day with any type of oil available confers great merit on him.

He who has *darshan* of this light on Arunachala Hill acquires the merit of having performed great charity and of having bathed in the sacred rivers. Who can express in words the benefits enjoyed by the one who has *darshan* of the peak of Arunachala with the beacon light glowing?

There is a story related to this festival:

Long ago, King Vajresan of Panchala who was childless, was blessed with a son after having *darshan* of the Arunachala *Deepam* in the month of *Kartika*. The son was named Shatrujith. The prince grew up to be a lecherous man. He once eloped with the wife of a *Vedic* scholar and came to Tiruvannamalai and entered the temple of Arunachaleswara. It was the day of the festival of the beacon. The paramour made a wick out of her saree and lit the lamp with castor oil. At that moment the *Vedic* scholar came there and in a fit of rage stabbed his wife and the prince. And in turn the prince killed him. Since it was a gruesome murder committed in the sacred precincts of the temple the three were about to be taken to hell by the messengers of Yama, lord of death. At that moment the messengers of Siva intervened and claimed the prince and the woman as their own and took them to the abode of Siva. Their blasephemous acts were condoned by Arunachala Himself because the wife made a wick and the prince helped her to light the lamp for the Supreme Lord. But the *Vedic* scholar was puzzled, as he was held by the messengers of Yama. The prince, moved by the plight of the *Vedic* scholar, offered the vessel used for lighting the *Kartika* lamp to release the scholar. Immediately the *Vedic* scholar was liberated. Thus all the three, despite their misdeeds, were taken to the abode of Siva, as the merit gained by the simple act of lighting a lamp on *Kartika* day in His temple, out-weighed their devilish acts.

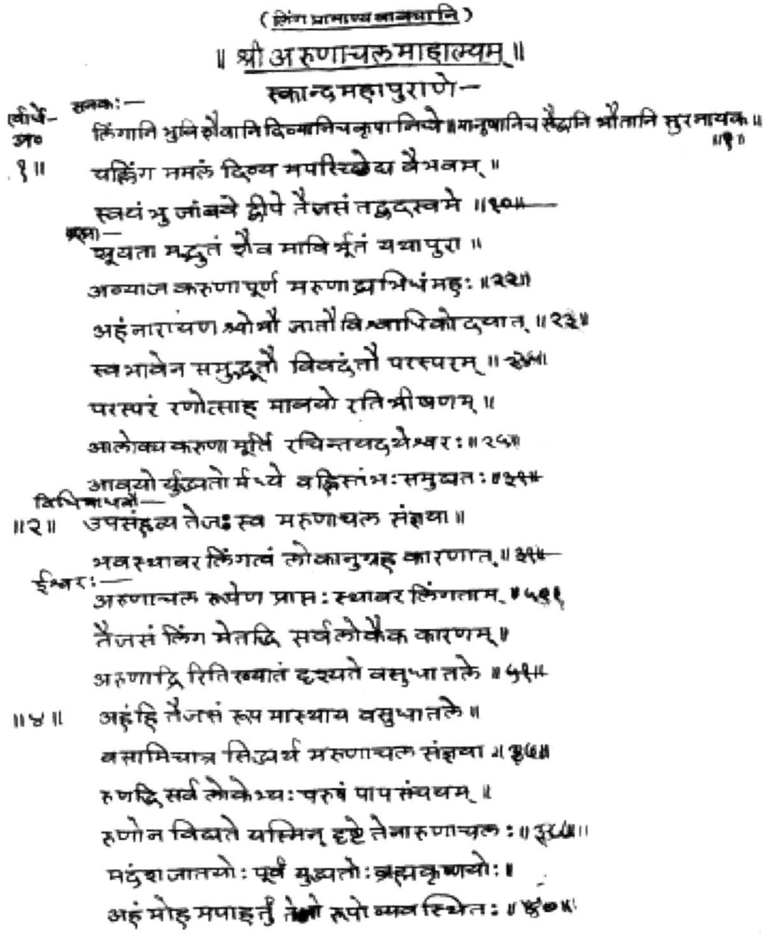


# Sri Arunachala Linga Pramanya Vakyani

IN 1938 the authorities of Sri Arunachaleswara temple filed a law-suit against the government regarding the ownership of Sri Arunachala Hill which was being claimed by the government as Forestry Department property. The temple authorities cited Bhagavan Sri Ramana Maharshi as a witness, and therefore on the May 8, 1938, the court sent a commission to hear Sri Bhagavan's evidence. [This incident is mentioned in Talk No 492 of *Talks with Sri Ramana Maharshi* compiled by Sri Munagala Venkataramiah.]

For the benefit of the court, Sri Bhagavan selected some passages from the *Skanda Mahapurana* and the *Siva Mahapurana* to prove that Arunachala Hill is itself a *Linga*, the very embodiment of Lord Siva[1]. In all he selected fifty-six lines from the *Skanda Mahapurana* and four lines from the *Siva Mahapurana*, and he copied these lines in a notebook[2] under the title *Sri Arunachala Linga Pramanya Vakyani* (statements giving authoritative proof that the Arunachala Hill is a *Linga*). On the basis of this evidence, the court decided that, since the Hill is itself a *linga*, it must be considered to be the property of the temple. The court also chose to recommend that the temple authorities allow the Forestry Department to make use of part of the Hill for forestry purposes.

The following is an English translation of the lines selected by Sri Bhagavan.

---

[1] The *Skanda Mahapurana* and *Siva Mahapurana* are two of the eighteen principal *puranas*, and as such they are recognized as works of great sanctity and authority. Therefore, when deciding an issue which concerns Hindu law, a court should abide by the authoritative statements made in these two works.

[2] This notebook contains the 292 verses about Arunachala which Sri Bhagavan copied from *Upamanyu Siva Bhakta Vilasa* at the time of this law-suit.

# SKANDA MAHAPURANA

## MAHESWARA KANDA, PART THREE
## (ARUNACHALA MAHATMYAM)
## FIRST HALF (PURVARDHAM)

## CHAPTER ONE

Sanaka said to Brahma:

9. O Treasure of Grace, O foremost among *devas*, on earth there are *Sivalingas* which are divine, which are installed by human beings and *siddhas*, and which are composed of the five elements.

10. Tell me, which *linga* in *Jambu-dvipa*[3] is immaculate (*amala*), divine (*divya*), of unmutilatable glory[4], self-originated (*swayambhu*) and Effulgent (*taijasam*).

*Brahma said:*

22. Hear how in ancient days the wonderful and effulgent Siva, who is full of motiveless grace (*avyaja karuna*), manifested with the name Arunadri.[5]

23. (first line). Narayana and I were born from Him (Sadasiva) who transcends the universe.

---

[3] *Jambudvipa*, the island of Jambu, is a name given to the land mass in which India is situated.

[4] The reading copied by Sri Bhagavan in this selection is *aparicchedya vaibhavam*, which means 'of unmutilatable glory'. An alternative reading is *aricchedana vaibhavam*, which means 'of a glory which destroys the enemies'. If the latter reading is taken, the word 'enemies' should be understood to mean the inner enemies, namely desire, anger, greed, delusion, pride and jealousy, together with their root, the ego.

[5] Arunadri is a name of Arunachala.

24. (first line). Once we two, who were self-born, began to argue with each other.

25. Seeing the the intensity with which we were fighting with each other, Iswara (Lord Siva), who is the embodiment of grace, then thought.[6]

31. (second line). He (Sadasiva) rose as a Column of Fire between us, who were fighting.

## CHAPTER TWO

Brahma and Vishnu prayed to Lord Siva

31. Withdrawing Your effulgence, abide as a motionless *Linga* named Arunachala in order to bestow grace upon the world.

*Brahma said:*

50. (second line). He (Lord Siva) assumed the nature of a motionless *Linga* in the form of Arunachala.

51. This indeed is the effulgent *Linga* (*taijasam lingam*), the sole cause of the universe, which is visible on earth and which is renowned as Arunadri.

## CHAPTER FOUR

*Isvara said:*

37. I truly abide here on earth in the form of an effulgence named Arunachala for bestowing liberation.

---

[6] What Lord Siva then thought is given in verses 26 to 30, which do not form part of this selection. A translation of these verses may be found in *The Mountain Path, April 1970*, p.66.

38. Since this Hill removes the heap of sins from all the worlds, and since bondage (*runa*) gets annihilated when one sees it, it is named Arunachala.[7]

40. In ancient days, when a fight arose between Brahma and Vishnu, who were both born from a part of me, I manifested myself in the form of an effulgence in order to remove their delusion.

43. At their further request I, who was in an effulgent form, became the motionless *Linga* named Arunachala.

## CHAPTER FIVE

Devi said to Gautama:

24. Siva told me, "I abide on earth as Arunachala," and said that I should hear the glory of Arunachala from your lips.

Gautama said:

42. (second line) and 43 (first line). In ancient days Brahma and Vishnu, who had come into existence from a part of the Effulgence of Siva, but who had become egoistic, fought with a desire to conquer each other.

43. (second line) and 44. In order to subdue the pride of these two, who were fighting in this manner, Sadasiva, who is meditated upon by *yogis*, assumed the form of a Column of Fire without beginning, middle or

[7] *A-runa-achala* means the Hill (*achala*) which makes bondage (*runa*) non-existent. This verse has been rendered into Tamil by Sri Bhagavan as the fourth of the seven verses on the greatness of Arunachala, which he adapted from the *puranas*. The literal meaning of Sri Bhagavan's Tamil rendering, which is an elaboration upon the meaning of the original Sanskrit verse is as follows: 'Since their nature is to bind all the worlds, the vicious actions (*karmas*) are bondage (*runa*). This Hill indeed is the Effulgent Arunachala (the Hill that destroys bondage), the refuge, by seeing which they (the *karmas*) vanish."

end, and stood between them illumining the ten directions.

47. At their request, Devesa (Lord Siva, the Lord of *devas*) assumed the form of a motionless *Linga* renowned as Arunadri and He now shines in all the *jivas*.

## CHAPTER SIX

Isvara said:

21. (first line). I abide on earth in the form of Arunachala.

22. (second line). That Effulgent Form[8] alone is called Arunachala.

23. This Effulgent Form, which is fiery, unmanifest and of the nature of limitless glory, has cooled down in order to protect the world.

## CHAPTER SEVEN

The *devas* said:

9. O Bhagavan, O Arunadrisa, O you who do good to the whole world! Although you are of the form of fire, shining in the world.

Gautama said:

5. Having been prayed to by the *devas*, Arunadrisa gradually cooled down and became perfectly tranquil as Arunachala in order to protect the world.

---

[8] The reading copied in this selection by Sri Bhagavan is *taijasa rupam*, which means 'Effulgent Form'. An alternative reading is *taijasa lingam*, which means 'Effulgent *Linga*'.

## CHAPTER EIGHT

20. (first line). You (Lord Siva) are seen on earth as the famous Sonadri[9].

17. (first line). Nowhere else on earth have I seen even one *linga* in the form of a Hill.

## CHAPTER THIRTEEN

Brahma said:

43. This is Sadasiva Himself in the form of Arunachala, which is seen as the Supreme Effulgence, the cause of creation, sustenance and dissolution.

44. This Effulgent *Linga* is worshipped by all the *devas*. Because of that (the existence of this *Linga* on earth), the *karmabhumi*[10] is considered to possess more *dharma* than any other world.

# SECOND HALF (*UTTARARDHAM*)

## CHAPTER FOUR

Nandikesvara said:

12. There God, Sambhu, the One who does what is good for the world, has Himself assumed the form of a Hill and abides as Arunachala.

14. This Hill, which is Parameswara Himself, is considered by *Maharshis* to be superior to Meru, Kailasa and Mandara.

---

[9] Sonadri is a name of Arunachala.

[10] *Karma bhumi* is a name for this earth.

58. (second line) and 59. Neither Meru nor Kailasa nor Mandara are equal to Arunadri, because they are abodes of Lord Siva made up of huge rocks, whereas this (Arunachala) is Girisa[11] Himself.

## CHAPTER SIXTEEN

Siva said:

27. For the welfare of the world, may my Effulgent Form, which is motionless and eternal, abide here forever with the name Arunadri.

## CHAPTER TWENTY

Gautama said:

21. (first line). This Arunadri is the Hill of Fire itself in a concealed form.

*Siva Mahapurana*
*Vidyeswara Samhita*

## CHAPTER NINE

Isvara said:

21. Since this *Linga* rose up as a Hill of Fire (Analachala), it shall be renowned as Arunachala (the Red Hill).

41. (Second line) and 42 (first line). Since this formless column (*nishkala stambham*), which reveals my *Brahmatva* (my nature as Brahman), possesses the characteristics of a *linga*, it shall be my *Linga*.

[11] Girisa (the Lord of the Hill) i.e. Lord Siva.

# Sri Arunachala Puranam: Vignettes

By J. Jayaraman

THE *Arunachala Purana* is an exquisite original composition in Tamil verse, by Saiva Ellappa Navalar who lived about three hundred years ago during the reign of the Tanjavur Nayaks. It enjoys the status of a *Sthala Purana* in Tamil on the 'story' of holy Arunachala (Tiruvannamalai).

*Sthala Puranas* record divine events, royal deeds and people's piety, all relating to a particular *sthala*, region. The incident of Lord Siva appearing as a column of light, thus baffling the forces claiming absolute doership, is perhaps the primal (and eternal) act of Grace; for it contains Time itself in its womb. This story finds mention in some form or the other in Vedas and various *Puranas*.

Specific references to Arunachala occur in various Sanskrit texts of antiquity. In the year 1938 a question arose as to whether the Holy Arunachala Hill came under the jurisdiction of the Arunachala Temple or the Government. The temple authorities approached Sri Bhagavan and requested him to depose before a tribunal regarding this matter. It was in this context that the Maharshi gathered references to Arunachala from five sources in Sanskrit and copied out the 2659 verses in his own hand. This Sanskrit collection, which may be called *Arunachala Mahatmya*, was translated into Tamil prose and and published by Sri Ramanasramam in 1957 under the same name.

The five major Sanskrit sources are given below:

1. The *Skanda Mahapurana*, one of the eighteen great *puranas*. It consists of a hundred thousand verses, each of thirtytwo syllables. They are distributed among six *Samhitas* of which *Rudra* (Sankara) *Samhita* alone has thirty thousand verses. The *Maheswara Khanda* is one of the twelve *Khandas* (divisions) of this *Samhita*. The third *Kaanda* (Part) of this *Maheswara Khanda* treats of Arunachala Mahima. This major text, rendered into Tamil verse by Saiva Ellappa Naavalar, forms nearly the first half of *Arunachala Purana*.[1]

The greatness of the sacred spot, the contest between Brahma and Vishnu, the destruction of Daksha's sacrifice by an angry emanation from Siva, the wedding of Siva and Parvati, Her playful sport and Her *praayaschitta* by

[1] The latter portion of this Tamil *Purana* is translated from *Linga Purana*. The poet mentions this fact in the beginning of the latter portion. Bhagavan's court deposition also mentions that *Linga Purana* contains references to Arunachala. However, the *Arunachala Mahatmyam*, compiled by Bhagavan, does not include *Linga Purana* references. Presumably the Sanskrit text of the *Purana* was not available.

penance, the destruction of Mahishasura, the merger of Parvati in Siva's left half, the greatness of *pradakshina* of the Hill, the Grace accorded to kings Vajraangada Paandya, Ballaala Chera and Pradatta, and the story of the civet cat are all narrated here.

2. *Siva Rahasya*, an *itihasa* nearly as long as the *Mahabharata*, contains twelve *amsas*. (This *Siva Rahasya* is different from the work of the same name which is in *Skanda Mahapurana*). The sixth *Amsa* (portion) of this contains the incomparable *Ribhu Gita*. The ninth *Amsa* contains references to the Saint Jnanasambandha's hearing of the greatness of Arunachala when he camped near it.

3. The *Vidyeswara Samhita* of *Siva Mahapurana* refers to the significance of worshipping Siva alone as Linga, in addition to the *vigraha* (idol) worship by which all gods are extolled. There are references to *lingodbhava*, and the five *krityas* — activities — of Sadasiva, viz., Creation, Maintenance, Destruction, Delusion and Grace.

4. The *Vidyaasaara Samhita* of *Siva Mahapurana* has a reference to the immense efficacy of feeding the poor in Arunachala.

5. The *Kshetra Khanda* of *Skanda Upapurana* (a minor *Purana*), speaks of incomparable benefits of observing vows during the month of Kartigai, and the attainment of *Mukti* by any one who has a glimpse of the Holy *Deepam* on that day.

The first of the above five and also a portion from *Linga Purana* were translated into Tamil verse by Saiva Ellappa Naavalar a few hundred year ago during the reign of the Tanjore Nayaks. Running to 649 verses, it is known as ARUNACHALA PURANAM. It excels the original in many a place, especially where the poet revels in a description here or brings to light there a subtle point easily ignored by the reader in the original. In addition, the metre changes now and then, providing instantaneously the atmosphere and rhythm which blend with the events the poet seeks to convey through words. It is hoped that a reader not acquainted with Tamil would get a taste of the *Puranam* through these vignettes.

After the verses offering prayer to Ganesha and Nataraja, the poet extols Arunachala as the fertile and sacred region where the Suns and Moons, the *Bhairavas, Vidyaadaras, Devas*, and those in charge of the Eight Directions, the *Nagas*, great *Tapasvins* and *Munis*, and Brahmas and Vishnus gather in such proximity that there is no place left to prostrate, and so their wave-like cry of "Hara, Hara!" drowns even the roar of oceans. The spectacle of the youthful women of this place, tender breasted, with pleasing mien, and ornament on either ear, makes one wonder whether a shining, cool, ambrosial moon (their face) had arisen in day-time accompanied by two suns (two ear-ornaments)!

Then follow verses praising Arunachaleswara (Siva), Unnamulai Amman (Parvati), Ganesa and Subrahmanya. These are followed by obeisance to the Tamil saints and finally to Nandi, Durga, Rishi Gautama and Chandikeswara. The poet then ridicules his own attempt at singing a few songs in the presence of eminent pandits skilled in composing songs pregnant with the eight

*Rasaas*[2]. He likens his bravado to that of a mosquito trying to show a thing or two about flying, in the presence of the Swan, mount of Brahma, and Garuda, mount of Vishnu.

The wise, however, would accept without ridicule his feeble attempts, because Arunachala is the theme of the songs, the same way as water by virtue of admixture with milk becomes elevated; or as a common thread becomes acceptable by virtue of being strung through fragrant flowers.

## On the Glory of the Arunachala Sthala:

Once, the sage Maarkandeya, leading a group of *Rishis*, prayed to Nandikesvara to tell them about easy ways to cross the Ocean of *Samsara* and reach *Mukti*. The Lord deigns to reply that a dip in the holy Ganges at Kaasi (Benares) done in full faith, or shedding one's mortal coils there; being born in Tiruvaaroor (Kamalaalaya); a glimpse of the Dance of the Three-Eyed One at Chidambaram; a visit to Vriddhaachalam where Vishnu offered worship to Siva and received the *Chakra* as boon; a pilgrimage to Kedarnath; *Darsana* of the Lord at Mallikaarjuna whom Brahma worships prior to every creation — all these are ways to *Mukti*. Further, there is Kaalahasti where Siva stands as a hill in order that Vishnu, wearer of the fragrant *Tulasi* garland, and Lakshmi, resident

---

2 Romance, Valour, Humour, Compassion, Ferocity, Disgust, Wonder and Fear.

of the cool, honey-dripping Lotus, may have His direct *Darsana* from their holy abode on the Tirupati Hill. Not only that, He also resides on the hill of Kaalahasti as the *Linga* worshipped of yore by the hunter-saint Kannappar. Further there are Kaanchipuram of great renown, Kumbhakonam, Seerkaazhi, Madurai, Rameswaram and many more which lead to *Mukti* by mere virtue of birth or death there, or by worship of the Lord therein.

Hearing these words of Nandikesvara, Maarkandeya addressed him as follows: Visiting these diverse places and offering worship and engaging oneself in allied activities is quite a task even for the long-lived gods and *siddhas*. What then can mortal men hope to gain in a life-span brief as a flash of lightning? Worse still is the plight of animals and birds, and hopeless indeed the fate of trees and shrubs. I request you therefore to enlighten us about a place with power to grant Release not only for trees, beasts and birds, but also for the old, the infirm and the lame among men for whom bathing in rivers, *pradakshina*, ritual worship and *namaskara* are out of the question. Please enlighten us about such a place in which any *jiva* could be confident of *kaivalya*, Release.

When thus the Sage Maarkandeya, the vanquisher of Death, worshipped with the other sages the Lotus-feet of Nandikesvara, the Lord raised his palm in benediction as if to say: "I shall tell you!" However the very remembrance of Arunachala in his Heart, prior to his uttering that word, struck Nandikesvara himself speechless in non-dual Bliss! He sat still for long, with palms joined as if in prayer, hair standing on end all over the tingling body, with tear-filled eyes, and in a trance. Then as if awakening, he sang forth: "O Lord of Arunagiri, wearing the Ganges in your matted hair! O Lord of Flaming Eyes, who ever overwhelms us with your Grace!" He then proceeded to address the sages: "Listen. There is a place on earth which grants Deliverance to any created being, moving or unmoving, by the mere rememberance of its sacred name. It has innumerable names. Some of these are: Gowri Nagara, Tejo Nagara, Arunachala, Sivaloka Nagara, Mukti Nagara, Jnana Nagara, Sthaleswara (the Supreme among sacred spots), Suddha Nagara, Dakshina Kailasa (Southern Kailasa), Sonagiri and so on. Being the Spiritual Centre of Creation it draws the gods, sages and *Tapasvins*, in short anyone who thinks of it, to itself. There is a Hill there which stands in *Krita Yuga* as a Hill of Fire, in *Treta* as one of Diamond, in *Dvaapara* as a Golden Hill and in *Kali Yuga* as a Hill of Stone. When even Vishnu as a boar and Brahma as a swan had to abandon their long-drawn search to find its beginning and end, can we hope to find a Hill to equal Arunachala? The Sun, thirsting to sip from the springs on this Hill, the water of which even the celestial Ganges considers holy directs his chariot-horses to leap over Arunachala daily! When dense clouds of white surround its base, it appears as though Arunachala were a rising peak amidst a snow-clad Himalayas! To cap it all, the *Deepam* which is lit on its summit during the cool month of Kartik seems like a prominent diamond on a grand crown worn by Mother Earth. Why, even

Himavaan, the god of the Mountains, was once crest-fallen that he had to give his daughter Uma in marriage to a mendicant, the skull-carrying Siva. But leaping with joy when informed of how Siva had once silenced Brahma and Vishnu by assuming the form of a Hill, Himavaan exclaimed with obvious relief, "How wonderful to know that our son-in-law-to-be belongs to our race after all!"

Reiterating the greatness of Arunachala, Nandikesvara tells the assembled sages that even murderers, those of easy virtue, or the disabled and those that live far away, are assured of *Mukti* if they but remember well the holy Arunachala once. The place is Sivaloka itself and its every pebble the holy Linga; every tree and shrub there is a wish-fulfilling *kalpaka* tree; every spring therein is the holy Ganges issuing forth from the matted tress of Siva; to eat a morsel there is to partake of the *amrta* of gods; a mere perambulation of it is *pradakshina* of Earth itself. Any sound uttered therein is to utter *Sruti* profound! Need we add that even to sleep there, is to be in *samadhi* supreme? Abandon therefore any possibility of finding an equivalent to Arunachala!

Saying these words of praise Nandikesvara remained still, where seated, immersed in Bliss. The sages prostrated again and again to the Lord, themselves lost in it.

Then Maarkandeya, son of Mrkandu, came forward and begged the Lord to narrate to them all, how the Arunachala Hill came to be formed. Nandi was pleased to say, "If a wretch should contemplate committing the *pancha paatakas*, (the five sins of murder, theft, falsehood, intoxication, and abuse of Guru)[3] in that sacred place, he would purely by virtue of his remembrance of "Arunachala", be saved somehow, and led to Liberation. Such is the undisputed sanction of the sacred scriptures. Would this Supreme Grace be then withheld from those devoted, who seek to hear more and more about the Holy Hill? The benefits are assured for my own self too!"

In what follows, Nandi describes Involution of *Samsaara*, as the process of merger of Brahma into Vishnu into Rudra into Maheswara into Sadasiva. This entity in turn relapses into *Bindu* that into *Naada*, and finally into *Sakti* which is Awareness inseparable from Being, called Supreme Siva, Parama Siva, *Srishti Krama*, the process of Evolution, appears in reverse, due to the very nature of Supreme Being. During such an Evolution, when Brahma appeared, he held in mind the idea of "many". Almost instantaneously the *Prajaapatis*, progenitors of races, came into being. Through them arrived in ordered succession the races of *Aadityaas* (Gods); *Daityaas* (*Raakshasaas*), and *Daanavaas* (the demonic races of *Asuraas*); the intermediate beings called *Kaalakeyaas*, *Gandharvaas* and nymphs, *Garudaas*, *Panis* (serpents), *Kinnaras*, and Anthropoids and the great races of *Rishis* and Humans.

All this creation taking place by his mere contemplation of it, was sufficient to turn Brahma's (many) heads. Puffed up with the pride of omnipotence that

---

[3] Murder: To ascribe birth to oneself. Theft: Illegal appropriation of false individuality. Falsehood: To believe "I am this limited, evolving body-mind". Intoxication: Self in search of happiness and Self-realization. Abuse of Guru: Not surrendering individuality while prostrating to Siva or Self.

seemed to be his, he decided to put Vishnu in his place once and for all! (This was undoubtedly an oft-repeated occurrence throughout the cycles of Creation. Forgetfulness of one's Source has a lot to do with this, surely. For, there are other accounts of a nascent Brahma venturing out of the Lotus in which he found himself. After climbing over many a row of petals and then sliding a while down its seemingly endless stalk, he soon lost courage. Vishnu, from whose navel the divine Lotus grew in the first place, restores Brahma to his 'abode' with full paternal concern. It was a very grateful Brahma who went ahead with Creation on that occasion!) But things were obviously very different now.

Deciding to take matters into his own multiple hands, Brahma confronted Vishnu, as the latter lay on his Bed of Snake, and taunted him thus: "It is very clear to me now, that I am the cause of all this Creation that is taking place. So abandon any idea you may have that you are my Parent. If it were not for my act of Creation, you would be unemployed! Useless!" Vishnu spoke out: "My dear son! It does not befit you to talk disrespectfully to your Parent." Brahma, inflamed, let forth much abuse: "Enough of this. Give up rightaway the hallucination that you are the Great Preserver! Otherwise I shall create another one and entrust him with your job." When Vishnu replied rather casually as if tolerating an errant junior, Brahma blew up in anger. "Oho! So you seem to have forgotten that the wonderful Ocean on which you reside is merely the accumulated sweat of my toils. Better hide yourself in it before the

Cosmic powers that I might well create, surround you and destroy you! By such foolish ignorance you incurred the wrath of the great Rishi Bhrigu, and by his curse had to take repeated births. Ingrate, have you forgotten that all this only added to my work? Did I not have to create for the sake of every *Avatara* of yours, a body that suited you? Look at my hands blackened by all that needless toil!" Hearing these words, Vishnu replied that, for one born of a mere lotus which had sprung from his navel, Brahma was making too much noise. Brahma then let loose another torrent of scorn: "O Vishnu! Have you forgotten that you sprang from a mere pillar once. A worse beginning if you ask me! Pray tell me, was that pillar your father or was it your mother? I shall accept you as my parent if you have no hesitation in accepting the inert pillar to be your parent! Even if I do concede that you are my father, why should I dance to your tune? Don't you know that fire which springs from rubbing bamboo sticks, burns up the parent sticks? So behave yourself lest I should destroy you!"

Hearing these wicked words Vishnu felt as if red-hot spears had been driven through his ears. With mounting anger he laughed spewing smoke, and after some thought replied, "Foolish fellow! You have neither bothered to enquire about your origin, nor shown inclination to accept my navel as your mother. Perhaps you assumed that as your parent I would tolerate any amount of mischief from a toddler like you. Beware! There is a limit to everything. The *asuras* Madhu and Kaitabha opposed me, and, though they were born of my body-sweat, I destroyed them. One cannot show mercy even if it be one's own child that did wrong. Does anyone shy from surgically removing a painful boil on one's own body? It is indeed comic that you consider yourself to be at the head of all creation, when you are unable to fashion for yourself a head and replace it — the fifth head, once plucked by Siva! Is it with these unenviable credentials that you set about creating this world, which after all is held aloft by Adisesha, my servant? And have you forgotten so soon that you squealed for help when an *Asura* ran away with the Vedas, and it was I who came to your rescue? I took the form of a fish then, out of my own sweet will. Innumerable have been the times when I have rushed to your succour by routing the *Daanavas* whenever they tormented you. One who has planted a tree is reluctant to uproot it even if it turns out to be a poisonous one. Though I hesitate on account of your being my son, I shall have to punish you if you persist in your invective."

Can fire subside by adding fuel to it? The exchange of hot words culminated soon in each drumming on his own chest, and the two circling each other like ferocious wrestlers, now advancing, now retreating, now leaping to the ground, now getting close, and goring each other with gimlet-eyes aflame with anger. All of creation went hay-wire. Mountains crumbled to powder, galaxies blew up in explosion, hot suns and cool moons disappeared enmasse. Rivers turned dry in a trice, stars and nebulae scatterred like confetti and the guardians of the Eight

Dimensions (*Ashta Dik Paalakaas*) feared the worst. Even the gods, who are of steady gaze, found themselves wincing, shocked by this sudden cataclasm. The fight for supremacy took a higher pitch with the combatants delivering blows to each other in the cosmic Arena. Punching each other, lifting the fallen one by his thighs and twirling him rapidly before throwing him far and high, the two, near equals, kept switching roles of victor and vanquished. The rise and fall of the dark-hued Vishnu and bright-hued Brahma looked like night following day amidst a pugilistic pell-mell.

The sequel is well: the sudden appearance of a blazing Column of Light growing beyond the seven planes below and the seven above; the search for its limits by the proud pair, which reminds one of an ignorant child reaching out to grasp the moon reflected in the water, Brahma's lie; the eventual humbling of the two by the appearance of Siva from the effulgence; His command proscribing all worship of Brahma on earth, and His appeasement by the contrite couple, who sing His praise.

## On the Holy Descent of the Divine Mother:

Nandikesvara continued: Listen, O Maarkandeya! I shall tell you how the divine Mother, Sati, came to be born as Parvati, daughter of Himavaan, the King of hills, and how She was wedded to Siva, the non-dual One, and how She came to be born on earth.

**The Episode of Sati:**

Daksha, the progenitor born of Brahma's right-thumb, was never too happy about the skull-carrying Siva whom fate had decreed to be his son-in-law. He bore a grudge ever since the latter had paid him, his father-in-law, no special attention and respect in an august assembly where he had been Siva's guest.

Soon he organised a *Brhaspatisavana* sacrifice, inviting all the Twelve, the Eleven, the Eight, and the Seven[4] and also the Serpents, *Kinnaras*, *Yakshas* and *Siddhas*, and a host of sages. Vishnu and Brahma were there with their consorts. Behold, my Lord Siva and Sati, being uninvited, were absent. When Sati expressed to Siva Her wish to attend Her father's great *Yaga*, sacrifice, the Lord replied that they had not been invited. But knowing well what was to follow, He smiled teasingly and said, "Go yourself, and come back soon!" She reached Her parents' place. Her warm embrace of Her mother Asikni was rebuffed. Her misguided father uttered words mean and mordant when She prostrated before him. Stung to the quick, Sati stormed out of the place but not before cursing the precincts and the participants to a moribund ravage. Elsewhere, the crescent moon on the matted locks of the One, ever Her other half, began to spew out heat, and out of His angered third Eye emanated a fierce form that sent shock-waves through space. Dark as a cloud, wearing an emerald crown, like a motile Meru mountain, mouthing thunder and spouting virulence, Veerabhadra appeared

---

[4] *Adityas*, *Rudras*, Directions, *Rishis*, respectively

with bloating body and twitching eye-brows before Siva, saying: "Command, command, command, my Lord!" Bidden to rout a rascally ritual, Veerabhadra sped thither; the mighty hordes, the *Siva Ganas*, close on his heels. With the hordes holding for him umbrellas pearl-studded, Veerabhadra went forth on a 100-bull-elephant-drawn chariot amidst the *Ganas* blowing war-calls from crores of Conches. Furious at the considerable slight to their Lord, the *Ganas* entered the *Yaagasala*. The Lords of the Eight Directions clashed with the irrepressible invaders. The field was but a blur of sword, spear, mace and guided missiles. With the leisurely ease of *Ammaanai*, a woman's parlour game, the *Ganas* made mince-meat of the *Devas* and their celestial vehicles. There was a tense moment when eight of the *Bhutas* fell and the rest stood in shock, but Veerabhadra cast eight projectiles which drank the life-blood of some gods and wounded the rest. The rider of the Cloud hopped off it in haste and took flight, changing himself into a cuckoo. In shame Nirriti, Varuna, Vaayu, Kubera and Isaana showed a clean pair of heels. Yama, lord of death, died. Agni, lord of the leaping flames, had his seven hands severed like the round of births by mere remembrance of Arunachala. Painlessly cutting away the ears of milady's mother with his laser-like Vajra, Veerabhadra confronted Daksha who rushed at him drunk with sacrificial Soma and wielding an uprooted pillar. It was a terrible scene, for the *Yajamaana*, the head of the *Yaga*, was himself beheaded. In a trice the head went rolling, and instantly, an impateint *Gana* went and gobbled it up!

Veerabhadra's work continued: his wielded trident left a trial of death where it went. The crowds of *Rudras*, *Maruts*, *Vasus* and the groups of *Rishis* hiding behind bushes or on trees — none, neither god nor goddess was spared. Veerabhadra and the *Ganas* routed the ritual and the ritualists, putting to flight divinities who had the temerity to attend a sacrifice to which their Lord, Siva, was not welcome.

Noticing that Brahma kept creating more gods, Veerabhadra cut off his hands, and impaled with the Trident the heads of the ten gods that Brahma, crippled in hands, had created through mind. That done, he took on Vishnu.

What follows may strike some devotees as irreverent. But we should not forget that the *Puranas* are united in their intent: that, however exalted a power one may be, there is a price to pay if ego emerges. And so, when Vishnu found his volley of arrows foiled by Veerabhadra, he threw a sword which the latter broke with an arrow that sped on to kill Garuda. With a face further darkened by the turn of events, Vishnu[5] hurled the space-warping Discus. Swifter than light, deadlier than death, it sped toward Veerabhadra, and took refuge at his feet. Had not Vishnu once offered worship of a thousand choice flowers to Siva, and at the very end of it, finding himself short of a flower, readily offered his own lotus-eye? Had not Siva presented him then with this *Chakra*, discus? What wonder then? Vishnu vanished, reappearing as a boar, then a lion and

[5] As Krishna, he is already dark.

so on. Veerabhadra's weapons proving invincible, he hid himself as a fish deep in the ocean's bowels. He who had once swallowed the earth[6] once again did it, hiding in its bowels. When Siva heard of all that had happened through Veerabhadra, His anger was quenched. The lesson taught, He revived all who had fallen prey to His wrath, and restored each to his *status quo ante bellum*. What of Daksha and Sati? He who begot Sati got a goat for his head. Sati, unable to bear the shame of being called daughter of the one who insulted Her Lord, had already taken Her life by Her *yogic* will.

## The Episode of Parvati:

Sati was reborn as the lovely child of Himavan (Lord of the Himalayas) and Mena, in answer to their *Tapas* and prayer for a daughter who would marry none other than Siva. How can I describe greatness of the *Tapas* of Himavan and Mena which brought forth Sakti? The Sakti which, while ever remaining as *Paraa* united with Siva, also springs forth as Creative Energy *Aparaa*, giving birth to the Seer-Seen duo and the Knowledge-Will-Action (*Jnana-Iccha-Kriya Sakti*) trio. The Sakti from which pure Maya gives birth to the potential and the manifest, the Implicate and the Explicate, the Nada and the Bindu. The Sakti, the primal seed from which sprout powers of Cosmic Management (called Brahma, Vishnu and Rudra). Oh! The *Tapas* of Himavan and Mena to have given birth to

---

[6] A *leela* of Krishna.

the Womb of all creation before and after! Lovelier by the day the lass grew, like the waxing moon, and like the sugarcane grown fondly by Kaama (Cupid) for enticing the three-eyed One some day. Naarada, knower of arts, sciences and the Vedas, came there one day, and informed Himavan that from certain marks that he had noticed in lovely Uma, it was certain that She would soon develop a half-eye on Her forehead, and a trident in one of Her hands. The breast on that side would gradually disappear. Half Her emerald-green body would turn coral-red, and half Her lovely hair would turn matted. Himavan who was overjoyed to infer from this that Uma was indeed the bride-to-be of Siva, was further elated when informed that Siva, the eternal Celibate, was for some mysterious reason performing *Tapas* very near Himavan's abode. (We however know that Siva somewhat dejected with the loss of Sati took to a life of seculsion and meditation). Offering his obeisance to Siva, Himavan bade Uma, assisted by Her friends, to remain there with the Lord and serve him with devotion. There were other developments elsewhere. The demon Taaraka, empowered by *Tapas*, was making a hell of heaven. A shocked Brahma found himself facing a highlevel team that looked quite downcast. Deprived of their godly crowns, there they stood: Indra with his broken *Vajra*, Isaana with his blunted Hatchet, Yama with his Trident twisted, and so on. "Taaraka. . ." was all that they could stutter, in reply to Brahma's query regarding the cause of their ignominy. Seized of the horrible threat from Taarakaasura to the gods, Brahma advised: Abandon any hope of saving the situation through individual efforts. This demon Taaraka had got the boon that he could be defeated only by a son born to Siva the eternal recluse. Rather clever of him. So busy yourselves conjuring up ways to consummate the marriage of Shailaja (hill-born Parvati) with the Celibate. Returning to Amaraavati, Indra had only to think of Manmatha, Cupid, when he appeared before him asking: 'Whose *Tapas* do you want disturbed? Which damsel do you want stricken with my Arrows? Why this sorrow-laden face?' Much depended on what Maara (Cupid) could do. Re-enacting the characteristic drama of new-found intimacy in times of distress, Indra embraced his friend Manmatha with both his arms, and according him an honoured seat, explained to him the role Maara had to play in enticing Chandramauli[7] from His austerities. Convinced that this was nothing short of asking for the moon, Manmatha explained: 'Who can disturb the *Tapas* of the One who is ever beyond epistemology (means of knowledge) in the form of sensation (*Pratyaksha*), mentation (*Anumaana*, inference), or citation (*Sruti*)? By the very *Sannidhi* (proximity) of the consummate Virgin and the faultless Celibate, creation emerges, stays, and merges, like thought-forms in Mind. Though He is described as *Tamasic*, His *Svarupa*, essential form, is Fire. He cannot be framed by form; nor can He, as formless, be circumscribed. Worse still, I could do my job only if I knew for sure that my target was a male or

---

[7] Siva with the moon in his matted locks.

that it was a female. Siva is neither male, nor female, nor both! I am sorry. It's beyond me to budge the Bull-rider.'

Realising that the situation called for drastic measures, Indra got up, and launched into heady adulation of Ananga's[8] prowess. 'Have you forgotten that it was by your amorous ammunition that Vishnu got Lakshmi seated in His breast, and Saraswati took residence on Brahma's tongue? Why! Was it not due to your virile greatness that even I, Indra, came to acquire a thousand eyes?'[9] Now clasping Kaama's arm with both his hands, Vajrabaahu[10] shot his bolt. 'Please go for *my* sake! Success with Siva spells birth of Skanda. And that means life again for all Devas. It is the supreme moment for you! Please do not refuse. Grant me this one boon!' Thus thoroughly seduced, Kaama sped to Kailas, to move the Immovable. Armed with bow made of sugar-cane strung with a row of bumble-bees serving as bow-string, and his quiver of just five arrows tipped with five fragrances, Maara marched on. Riding with his consort Rati, on Southern Breeze that served as his fish-flagged chariot, and with indulgent Spring as his Prime Minister, Kaama sped on. While the Moon wove its delicate web of lover's light, the cuckoos sang atop trees flush with flowers, and amidst the buzz of bumble-bees, emanating as calls to war from conch-like white jasmines, and with flowers being strewn about in honey-dripping flood all along the road, the female

---

[8] Kama, the bodiless; called so here in tragic anticipation!

[9] Indra's caper with Ahalya earned him this curse from Gautama Rishi.

[10] Indra, wielder of the *Vajra*, thunderbolt.

warriors of Kaama, capable of melting even iron, copper and stone with their sweet talk, ambled on, holding in their hands, deadly harps that played on heart-strings. The romantic Night was Ananga's army of dark elephants; the twinkling stars were the silvery decorations on the faces and trunks of the elephants; and crimson sun-set the Bindi-dot adorning their foreheads. Parrots were the Cavalry, while warriors — dainty damsels with doughty breasts and coral lips sauntered on swishing their sword-sharp eyes.

Fearing a direct confrontation, Kaama hid himself out of view of the serenely seated figure of Siva and began to wonder what to do. He saw Uma approaching, and was suddenly filled with renewed confidence in having found a female accomplice. What was a crisis was now a cake-walk! As he bent his sugar-cane bow—the poet makes a delightful play on words here—Kaama thought, "Even if this bow of the form of sugar-cane, *karumburuvam* (Karumbu + uruvam)[11] be broken in the bargain, why should I worry? Have I not the black brows, *karumburuvam* (karum + buruvam) of Uma, to stand in as two more brows"! What followed this is history. As Kaama released the arrows, he was burnt to ashes by a ray from Siva's third Eye. Later, leaving that spot, Siva returned to Kailas and calling the sages to His side told them that Parvati was engaged in long *Tapas* for gaining Him as Her husband, and so He instructed them to go to Himavan and inform

---

[11] *Buruvam* (also pronounced as *puruvam*) is the Tamil for the Sanskrit *bhruva* (Brow).

him that Siva was happy to seek Her hand in marriage. Himavan and his family were thrilled to hear of this. The auspicious date for the Supreme alliance was fixed and communicated back to the Lord. Soon invitations were despatched to the near and dear—the seven (kinds of) hills, the seven Oceans, *Devas*, *Siddhas* and *Rishis*. Soon thereafter the Oceans, the garland-like meandering Rivers, the Blue-mountain (Nilgiris) and other ranges, and *Siddhas* and *Munis* and *Devas* began to arrive. The Eight directions on earth were jammed with chariots and flags, the free space above was a packed parking-lot for aerial limousines. The streets were filled with garlands, festoons, and stumps of large-leaf plantains and areca palms planted as arches over doorways. The fragrance of the civet-paste obtained from the hills charmed the environs. The pomp and circumstance shamed Vishnu's Vaikuntha, Brahmaloka, Kubera's Alagaapuri and Indra's Amaraavati put together. The ladies of the hills bathed the Bride in the waters from Ganga. Her slim waist weighted with silken dresses, Uma was decorated with ornaments of pearl and gem and garlands of fragrant flower, and adorned with the *Kasturi Tilaka* on Her forehead. Siva, habitual wearer of the sacred ash, who scorched to ashes the flower wielding Smara (Kaama), now Himself was bedecked with flowers from the divine Kalpaka tree! Aided by Brahma and others, who clothed Him in habits studded with diamonds, Siva for once forsook from His neck and arms the fearsome Snakes that concealed lustrous diamonds in their heads (*maa mani ppanigal neekki*), and put on necklets and armlets of nine gems (*maa mani ppanigal pootti*). Then sporting a brilliant bejeweled crown that seemed as if the heavenly stars had all gathered at His tresses to be near their Master the crescent Moon, and wearing *kundalas* (large rings) that made it seem as if the Sun and Moon of His eyes had taken residence just below His ears, the resplendent bridgegroom mounted the Rishabha, Bull. When Vishnu, the best-man, came near and uttered words of praise, the Lord lovingly spoke to him; when Brahma, lord of the lotus-bloom, approached in respectful obeisance, he was greeted with a nod of the crown (that 'contained' the head of the Infinite); when Indra next came forward singing a paean of praise, Siva the Plenum of Stillness bestowed on him a special smile! The other gods followed, paying their obeisance. Had the crescent Moon, nourished by the Ganges hidden in His tresses, grown so large as to become the wide, white canopy held aloft above Him? Were the two *chowries* (whisk fans waved by royal attendants) the white spray of the Ganges and the Moon? As the Lord proceeded now towards Kailas, Vishnu, lord of Lakshmi, followed with the betel-bag, Indra, king of the celestial Kalpaka, carried the Taambula-vessel to receive the red remains, Brahma fanned, while Naarada's sweet strains and the drone of his divine *Tambura* floated afar. Yama was just a wee bit behind bringing the wooden Sandals, while Vaayu was busy burning *Saambraani* (incense of fragrant benzoin) and Isana duly carried in velvet the regal Sword. While Saraswati and Lakshmi sprinkled holy rose-water on all the guests, the divine damsels bore bags holding rare garments, the Naaga nymphs came carrying apparel sewn with all sorts of gems; and the *Kinnaras* playing on their lutes, and the Vidyaadaras singing in chorus "*Pallaandu, Pallaandu*" (Long live!), and the clang of cast bells, the rhythm of diverse drums, the crash of cymbals and solemn siren of conch was a *son et lumiere* truly for the gods! As the Lord rode through the city of Himavan, the women along the streets feasted their eyes on the One who would marry their princess. Some said: "Ah! Uma's *Tapas* has not been in vain." Some craned curious necks wondering: "Which is the eye of fury which burnt up Cupid?" Some others pronounced: "All the archery of Ananga (Kaama) is to no purpose really, for all of Creation remained placid to his passion as long as Siva remained in *Yoga*. On the other hand, even with Kaama no more, all are now aquiver with ardour merely by the Pinaakin[12] (Siva) bestirring himself to desire. Surely it is He who is the primal Cause of pining Passion!" Himavan leading his mountainous Family came forth and welcomed the Groom and his swelling crowds amidst much bonhomie and mutual embrace. With Brahma giving Him a helping hand, the Immeasurable, beyond beginning and end, alighted from the Bull-mount. The waving of saffron-water and light followed. Then, resting His right hand on both hands of the best-man (Vishnu), the Lord proceeded to the hall of marriage, and took the Groom's seat before the glowing Fire. With their ample breasts announcing their origins,

---

[12] Wielder of the Trident (*Pinaka*).

the maidens of the mountains conducted Kaali (Parvati the black beauty) the embodiment of Grace, as if She were a delicate flower, to the right side of Her consort. As the moment of Muhurta neared, Brahma progenitor of the Vedas, now as the chief Priest, voiced them once again. The Ritual came to a close when the Primal One offered puffed rice to the ghee-fed flames, and then, chanting the crucial *mantras* circumambulated the Fire (*his* own essence), holding the hand of the Virgin, Mother of the seven Worlds.

When the gods gathered to pay their obeisance to the newly-married, the Lord acquiesced to their combined entreaty, and, to the delight of Rati, resurrected Kaama from the ashes, now Ananga (bodiless). The Marriage over, the gods dispersed, each returning to his or Her station in the cosmic Scheme.

Ganesa and Subrahmania were born soon thereafter and while the gods, who had suffered long enough, watched in suspense, Subrahmania waged war with the redoubtable Taarakaasura and destroyed him with his valiant *Vale* (Spear).

## On the Blind-Folding of The Lord:

The Newlyweds would have tiffs, then make up; garland each other; listen to their praises sung by the *Rishis*; play on the Veena; dally in spirited sport or pass time in games, winning and losing them to one another. On one such occasion Parvati asked Her Lord, "Won't you tell me what the Moon and Sun are?" He replied, "Dear lass of lush Lips! The two lights are but my Eyes!" Thinking that he was teasing Her, the mother of Kartikeya went behind him and, without any warning, closed his Eyes. The momentary closure meant aeons of darkness for the gods. All of embodied life behaved as if born blind. Aye! Order and organisation broke down in the absence of the Eye-energy. In what was a trice for him, the Lord opened the Third Eye on his uncovered fore-head. The Destroyer had turned Life-giver! As Gauri drew Her hands back, the three Eyes shone like the three Vedic fires (*dakshina, gaarhapatya and aahavaneeya*) powering the 'unplanned' power-cut. When Parvati begged for forgiveness, Siva replied, "You are ever taintless and beyond *Karma*. However, if you desire to set an example of purification, go to Kaanchi which is greater than Kaasi, Avanti, Dwaaraka and Mathura." Narrations of the holy Mother's *Tapas* at various places are scattered throughout the Puranas. Was the Lord now advising Her of the superiority of Kaanchi over those places of Her earlier visits?

What follows is well known. From Kaasi Parvati reaches Kaanchi; makes a sand-Linga by the Kampa river and worships it day and night. The Lord wills a flood in order to test Her devotion. She embraces the *Linga* in protection unmindful of Her own fate in the spate. Pleased, the Lord appears before Her, "with his shoulders bearing the marks of the Paandya king's cane [13], his feet the marks of crowns of countless gods, his chest, embraced recently,

---

[13] See *Tiruvilaiyaadal Puranam.*

bearing the mark and sandal-scent of Parvati's breasts and bangles"! She requests for the ultimate boon of *Idappaaham*, of being his left Half. The ultimate asking; the *adviteeya*. The Ultimate, giving, said, "purified in Kaanchi, proceed now southward to holy Tiruvannamalai. Resident as the primal Linga contracted to a Hill, there I shall grant this boon!" Parvati, wise after the event, said, "Following your advice I came to Kaanchi 'superior to Kaasi'. And now you mention Arunachala! Please let me know right away if more places exist!" The Lord gave Her his word that the *Tejolinga* (Arunachala) is the Terminus.

*En route* to Arunachala from Kaanchi, Parvati encamped for the the night at Seyaar, the Son's River. It was here that Lord Subrahmania got a hut made of plantain trees for Her rest and the following morning enabled with a thundering arrow, a river of pure water to flow by for Her ablutions.

Passing then through paddy fields Parvati reached Tiruvannamalai. After obeisance to the Lord at the Temple to the east, She began to look for a spot to pursue *Tapas*. At the nearby Pavazha Kunru, Coral hillock, a spur of Arunachala Hill, She met the *Rishis* assembled at the Sage Gautama's *Ashrama* who sang the praise of Mother Parvati:

"Bringing forth the Eternal Siva from within you, you appear then within Him as the animating Sakti! With this, Thy mysterious nature (of Siva-within-Sakti-within-Siva), you procreate the multiple *jivas*. Is there anyone capable of finding out your nature which for ever remains non-dual!"

"If the Supreme Reality of Siva becomes Maheswara, Rudra, Brahma and Vishnu you become simultaneously the Saktis known as Maheshwari, Rudri, Saraswati and Lakshmi. Other than these should He assume any 'other', you *become* correspondingly. Is there anyone capable of knowing you!"

When the *Munis* and *Rishis* were praising Parvati thus, Gautama arrived, and coming near Her with hands raised above his head in supplication, prostrated before Her lotus-like feet.

Gautama, lofty in devotion, then addressed Her to Her delight, "What immense good have I done that Thy divine feet, that even Brahma (the First-born) and the *Ashta Dikpaalas* (the sentinels of the eight Quarters) cannot hope to place on their heads bowed low, should be gracing this most humble abode of mine!"

Hearing this, Parvati, gentle as a creeper, said, "Should need arise I shall go to the Spear-Wielder (Subrahmania), or the Tusker (Ganesa) to remove my want. Or else I shall come to you, dear son, who have such love for me."

She then related in detail all that had taken place till then during Her penance on earth. Hearing the Mother of all speak thus, Gautama who had (by a curse) bestowed on Indra, doer of a hundred *Yaagas*, in times of yore a thousand eyes, spoke as follows:

"This Abode, the primal One, is known as the Abode Supreme and is sacred *par excellence*. One good deed done here multiplies manifold of itself. Therefore do Thou conduct ardent penance here. Thy Lord will then surely come on His bull-mount and reabsorb you as His left Half."

"(O Mother) even Vishnu, Brahma, the Vasus, Indra, and a host of Munis had in days gone by, made their dwelling here and completed the penance of solitude. The place is right and the time auspicious. Thy penance is thus assured of success."

The sage Gautama told Her, "This holy place is ideally wooded for a radius of two *yojanas* (18 miles) and teems with life and life-giving streams. The distraction of crowds of gods and *siddhas* that frequent this Hill for worship has made me take shelter in the thick but secluded forest of this spur. Therefore do you too choose a spot nearby!" (The *Purana* indicates clearly that Gautama's *Ashrama* was at Pavazha Kunru to the east and that Parvati did *Tapas* near his *Ashrama*. This is also consistent with later events: She kills the demon and cleanses herself at the Khadga Tirtha which lies near the spur; She then begins, the *pradakshina* of the Hill from the east, and completes it there). Then the Mother Supreme, the Womb of all creation said, "Indeed I shall do *Tapas* here and gain my end."[14]

---

[14] For an incident highlighting Sri Ramana's *bhava* while reciting the above verses in Tamil, see *Guru Ramana*, S.S. Cohen's thrilling diary entry dated June 17, 1948.

# On the Episode of Obtaining Idappaaham, Merger:

Indeed the *aranyakas*, forests, are the fountain springs germinating and sustaining all that is best in Vedic wisdom and life. The Light of the Upanishad was communicated under the shade of the silent tree. Parvati began Her *Tapas* in the forest of Tiruvannamalai, then home to Nature's wild splendour. Could such magnificence escape the malefic marauder? The troops of the demon king Mahishaasura came from afar to capture the wild elephants, and to hunt for flesh and fancy the wild boar, bison, leopard and doe which roamed free in the forest, alert and aware. Mahisha's lusty letter to Parvati led to Her warning him, "This is the residence of those committed to the ideal of *Dharma*. Those who misuse their advantage to evil ends here, will lose their ease and die diseased, all their strength and authority wiped out. Do not incite Lord Arunachala, fiery by nature, towards anger, lest you should be destroyed. Beware!"

(The events that followed are well known and we shall confine ourselves to certain interesting aspects alone). In the battle that ensued, Mahisha, the buffalo-headed demon, proved redoubtable to Durga, the militant emanation from Parvati. When decapitated, the 'buffalo' took the form of a mad elephant. Beheaded, he went on successively taking the forms of a horse, of darkness and even appeared before Her as Brahma and Vishnu. Then Durga prayed to Uma in Her heart. The Supreme directed

Her to continue till the *Asura* assumed his *original* buffalo form. She was then to cut off his head and hold it under Her foot. Mahisha met his end thus. (Sri Ramana too prays in his *Arunachala Padikam*, verse 7, "Resident as I am in the non-dual Heart, who is it that comes out? Manifest thyself, O Arunachala; place Thy broad feet on his head, and subdue him!" Again, in Forty Verses, he declares Mahisha's secret, "It arises dependent and feeding on form; it abandons one form for another; when enquired into its original form, it is no more! Such is the formless ego-demon.")

After slaying Mahisha, Parvati went in *pradakshina* of the holy Hill. Half-way, near the west, the Lord gave *darshan* on his bull-mount. Her going round the hill was like Paarvati's earlier circumambulation of the sacred Agni on the day of Her Marriage! As She neared the east completing Her *pradakshina*, the Lord absorbed Her as his left-Half.

## On the Pradakshina of the Holy Hill:

(*prada* = giver of boons; *kshi* = destroyer of *Karma*; *na* = giver of *Jnana*. Also, *pra-dakshina* = going around with centre kept to the right). The holy Arunachala is the primal, *Adi Linga*. The path around its base is the sacred *Yoni*. *Pradakshina* of the Hill is therefore *pradakshina* of the source of all Lingas! So one goes round keeping to the left-edge of the path. A mere step taken, confers the benefit of a *Yaga*, sacrifice; two steps, the fruit of *Raajasuya Yaga*; and three that of *Asvamedha Yaga*. Going round the hill one gains in health and vigour. The hill abounds in rare herbs sought by *siddha* herbalists. The breeze carries the salubrious wafts from these *siddha* herbs to the one doing the holy round. The dust from the feet of such a person, carried and deposited in towns far away effects immeasurable purification.

The fruit of a Sunday *pradakshina* is Siva's abode; that of Monday is merger in Siva-form; that of Tuesday is termination of debt and cyclic death; that of Wednesday is divinity through skill in philosophy and art; that of Thursday is lordship over gods and god-men; that of Friday is lordship of the Lotus Lady. A Saturday *pradakshina* confers the astronomical benefits of a nine-planet Conjunction in the Eleventh House. The above effects are magnified if done on *Sivaraatri*, New-year day, or during the three months, mid-October to mid-January. The fruits increase by a factor of one crore if done on the two solstices; or on the day the moon is in the Magha asterism during February-March; or during the pre-dawn hour; or during solar eclipse, or *vidhipaada yoga*.

As to the ritual of the spiritual round, one abjures all thought of the opposite sex on the day of *pradakshina*. After bathing one wears clean white clothes, applies the holy ash and proceeds, giving alms but without accepting any. One does not wear shirt or shawl or carry an umbrella. Free from fear, anger, irritation or sorrow one walks on bare feet, without using vehicles. Without swinging one's arms about, with a silent soft tread, one saunters like a queen in her 'tenth-month'. One bows, first to the holy Hill from each of the eight cardinal Directions, and then to the Lord of that Direction enshrined in the *linga* there. One bows mentally to the incorporeal gods and *siddhas* going the rounds, and keeps to the side. One could keep silence of speech and mind; or one could allow thoughts to flow on to the Hill of Fire; or one could sing and listen to songs of devotional praise.

In the company of those of lofty character, one could halt here and there and enjoy a feast of fruit and milk. Otherwise, simple food free of flesh may be taken.

In conclusion, the *Arunachala Puranam* declares, "the residents of Tiruvannamalai must scrupulously follow the above rules. Pilgrims from far-away places are allowed to do the holy round according to their capacity."

ONE WHO READS OR LISTENS TO *ARUNACHALA MAHATMYAM* (GLORY OF ARUNACHALA) ENJOYS LONG LIFE, PROSPERITY AND HAS ALL HIS SINS WASHED AWAY AND ATTAINS THE LOTUS FEET OF LORD ARUNACHALA.